Contents

Preface

The subject of Roman forts, in Britain as elsewhere in the Roman world, is paradoxically both simple and complex. A superficial glance suggests that, from the later first century onwards, forts conformed to a standardized pattern: buildings are found in a more or less predictable arrangement within the tight confines of a neat, rectangular perimeter of defences. Yet a more prolonged look reveals a myriad of differences in detail between one fort-plan and another, as well as between the plan of one type of building in one fort and that of the same type in another. The mass of material available for study is, in fact, bewildering: over 240 Roman forts and fortresses are now known in Britain, and most of these have been at least summarily explored, although very few have so far yielded a plan of the entire layout. A full corpus is therefore badly needed; but it is the aim of this little book to do no more than give the beginner a flavour of the complexity of the subject. The notes and bibliography are for those who wish to delve further, but are in no way intended to be comprehensive. An asterisk in either text or notes indicates a place where the feature under discussion is still visible on the ground.

October 1979   R.W.

Note on the Plans

The plans, while drawn to scale, are schematic in that, for the sake of clarity, lines have sometimes been drawn thicker than is strictly accurate. In plans of fort defences, solid black denotes a rampart of earth with a timber breastwork, and a thin black line accompanied by grey tone indicates a stone wall backed by a mound of earth.

1

The Roman Army and the Roman Fort

The Roman Army

The years which separated Caesar's raids into Britain in 55 and 54 BC from the full-scale invasion under the Emperor Claudius in AD 43 witnessed a major turning point in European history. Out of the ruins of the Roman Republic and a bloody civil war emerged a man who, by delicate military and political manoeuvring, succeeded in establishing the principate as an institution and himself as Emperor. That man, born Cnaeus Octavius, became known to the world as Augustus, the title he adopted in 27 BC.

Among his many far-reaching reforms was a thorough re-organisation of the Roman army. Up to his time the regular fighting force was composed almost entirely of legionary soldiers, Roman citizens, the heavy-armed infantry whose skill and discipline had laid the very foundations of Rome's Empire. Increasingly, though, use had been made of other, non-Roman troops who were specialists in other branches of warfare, especially cavalry fighting.[1] These non-legionary regiments were known as auxiliaries (*auxilia*), and under Augustus they were re-organised as an integral part of the Roman army.

The distinction between legionary and auxiliary, at any rate during the early Empire, is an important one. The legionary was a Roman citizen from Italy, the auxiliary was enlisted from among the provincial peoples of the Roman Empire. The legionary was an infantryman and belonged to a legion with a nominal strength of 6,000 men. The auxiliary might be either an infantryman or a cavalryman and belong to a unit either 500 or 1,000 men strong. The legionary's base was a fortress covering about 50 acres; the auxiliary was stationed at a fort (*castellum*) which might vary in size from about two to seven or eight acres. Some of these distinctions became more and more blurred as the Empire wore on—for example, provincials were gradually enlisted in the legions from early in the second century. But the vast majority of the forts we shall be describing were never manned on a permanent basis by even a detachment of legionaries: a fort was normally designed to hold an auxiliary unit of the Roman army.

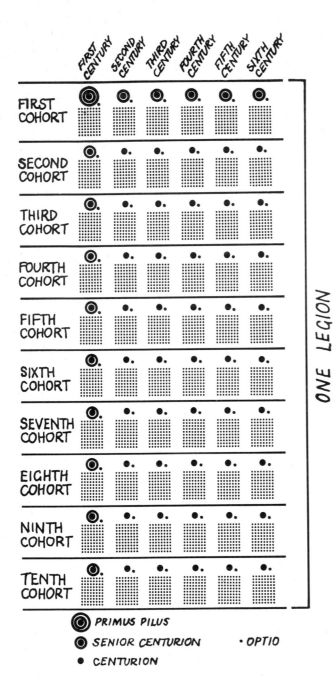

FIRST CENTURY · SECOND CENTURY · THIRD CENTURY · FOURTH CENTURY · FIFTH CENTURY · SIXTH CENTURY

FIRST COHORT

SECOND COHORT

THIRD COHORT

FOURTH COHORT

FIFTH COHORT

SIXTH COHORT

SEVENTH COHORT

EIGHTH COHORT

NINTH COHORT

TENTH COHORT

ONE LEGION

⊚ PRIMUS PILUS

◉ SENIOR CENTURION   · OPTIO

● CENTURION

1. Diagram to indicate the organisation of a legion in the early first century AD. Senior officers are not shown.

The organization of the legion and its chain of command are indicated in the accompanying diagrams. The basic unit was the century (*centuria*), consisting of 80 men at the beginning of the Empire; six centuries made up a cohort (*cohors*), and ten cohorts a legion (*legio*). All legionaries were infantrymen except for a cavalry contingent of 120 men whose names were carried on the books of the centuries. The officers of the legion were of two different types. The backbone of efficiency and discipline was provided by the sixty centurions, the tough professional NCOs who each commanded a century. Five of the six centurions of the First Cohort, and the senior centurions of the other nine cohorts, were senior in authority to the others (*primi ordines*), and they in turn bowed to the command of the legion's Chief Centurion (*primus pilus*), in charge of the first century of the First Cohort, and to the camp prefect (*praefectus castrorum*) above him. The job of camp prefect, the key man in the administration of the legion and responsible for all construction and repair work, was the summit of a professional soldier's career. Yet he had to answer to two other officers who were not even full-time military men. The legionary legate and the senior tribune were both of senatorial rank, one in his thirties, the other in his twenties, who held these army posts as part of a civil service career, which included civilian as well as military jobs. The five junior tribunes, also not professional soldiers, usually belonged to the equestrian order, a rank below that of senator which anybody of free birth could obtain by a property qualification. To us this system of putting civil servants at the head of a crack fighting force in the field might seem a little odd, but it was part of Rome's philosophy that a natural leader of men had equal potential in military as in civilian command, and the retention of this system until the fundamental changes of the late Empire is presumably an indication that it worked.

The picture is much less clear when we turn to the organization of the auxiliary units. Certainly by the middle of the first century AD there were three different types: the 'wing' of cavalry (*ala*), the most prestigious; the 'cohort' of infantry (*cohors*); and the part-mounted cohort (*cohors equitata*), which was a mixture of cavalry and infantry. All three were on paper 500 men strong in the mid-first century, although by the 70s double strength units had appeared. So much is clear: it is when we start investigating the internal composition that the problems occur. It is a fair guess that the infantry cohort of the auxiliaries was modelled on its legionary equivalent; in other words it contained six centuries of 80 men each, each commanded by a centurion and his second-in-command (*optio*). The cavalry regiment was divided into troops (*turmae*), not centuries, variously recorded as having 30 and 32 men each; but the latter figure probably includes the decurion in charge of each squadron and his second-in-command. The commander of each regiment, at first a tribal chieftain from the area where it was raised, was normally a civil servant of equestrian rank with the title 'prefect'.

The part-mounted cohort is the real problem. We know it had six infantry centuries and four *turmae* of cavalry, but if we presume the strengths of each were the same as in the centuries and *turmae* of unmixed units we have a total paper strength of 600, not counting the officers. This seems a bit high for a unit described as '500 strong' (*quingenaria*), so perhaps there were fewer men in each century and each *turma* in a part-mounted cohort. We can find a mathematically neat solution to the problem if we assume that the century was reduced in it from 80 to 60 men, making a basic total strength of 480 as in the other units, and support for this comes in a recently published third-century papyrus from Egypt.[2] This is not just simply a numbers game: we have got to know the size and composition of each unit if we are going to assign them forts to garrison, as clearly the type of accommodation needs to be different for the different units. The picture gets even more complicated when the thousand-strong regiments were introduced in the 70s (p 32).

What sort of men were these auxiliary soldiers? We have seen already that they were not Roman citizens: that was the award awaiting them on discharge after twenty-five years service. They were instead provincials, recruited as occasion demanded to form new regiments which took their names from the geographical or tribal area where they were raised, or occasionally from the name of the person responsible for raising them.[3] Once formed the regiment was sent to another province to do its service: that is why there are no 'cohorts of Britons' attested in Roman Britain.[4] But it is quite wrong for us to get the impression that the men who garrisoned the forts we will be describing were all foreigners from distant lands speaking a multitude of dialects: new recruits required for an already existing unit were drawn from the local population of the region where the unit was stationed. In other words any regiment which had been stationed in the province for a generation or so would have been composed more or less entirely of Britons, even though the regimental name and colours and even sometimes regional characteristics were carefully retained. Only very rarely did a unit continue to recruit from its original recruiting ground. One example is the specialist cohort of Hamian archers from Syria stationed at Carvoran on Hadrian's Wall.[5]

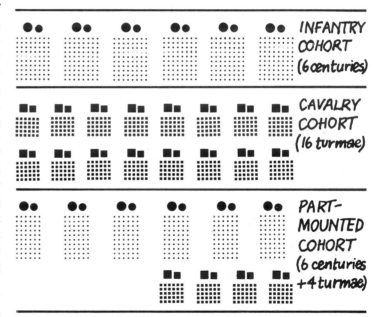

INFANTRY COHORT (6 centuries)

CAVALRY COHORT (16 turmae)

PART-MOUNTED COHORT (6 centuries +4 turmae)

● CENTURION
● OPTIO

■ DECURION
■ SECOND-IN-COMMAND

2. Diagram to indicate the organisation of the three different types of auxiliary regiment in the early first century AD. That of the part-mounted cohort is far from certain.

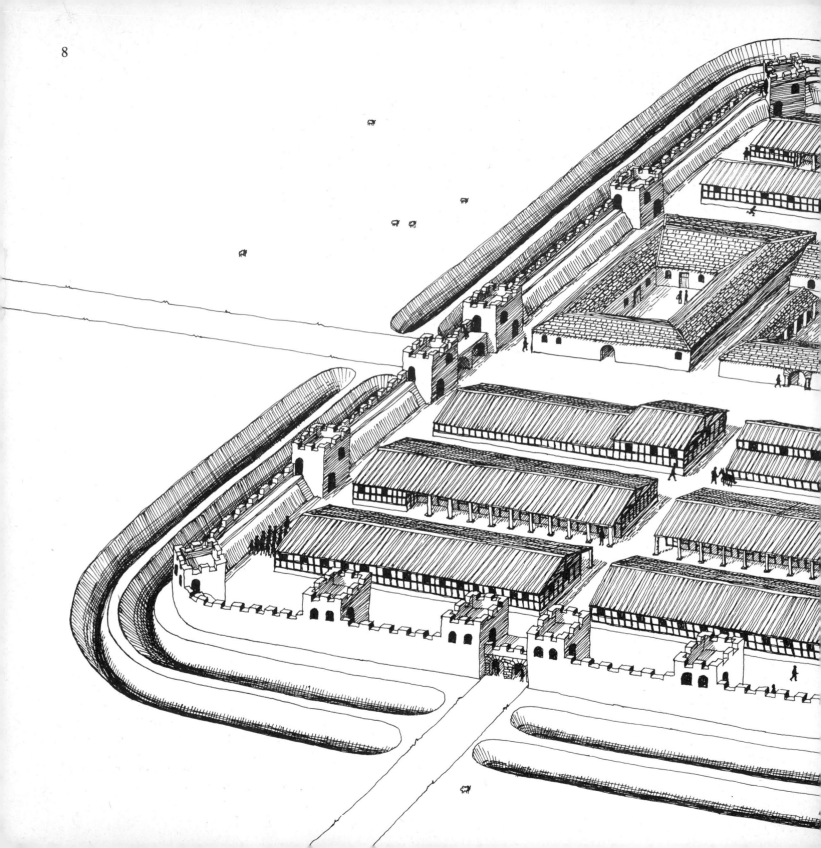

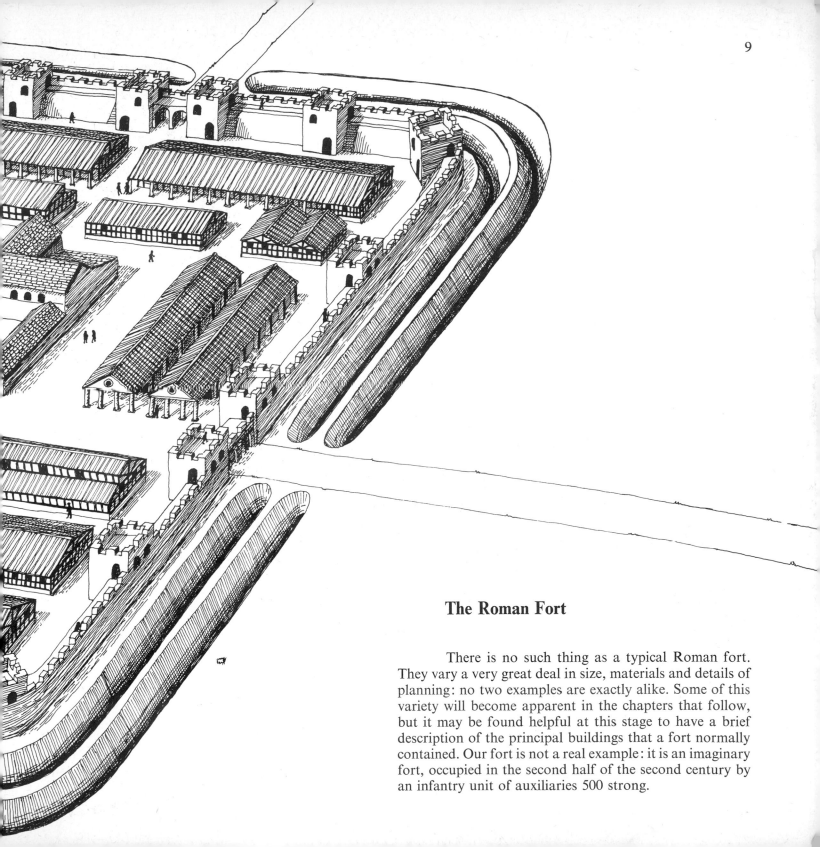

The Roman Fort

There is no such thing as a typical Roman fort. They vary a very great deal in size, materials and details of planning: no two examples are exactly alike. Some of this variety will become apparent in the chapters that follow, but it may be found helpful at this stage to have a brief description of the principal buildings that a fort normally contained. Our fort is not a real example: it is an imaginary fort, occupied in the second half of the second century by an infantry unit of auxiliaries 500 strong.

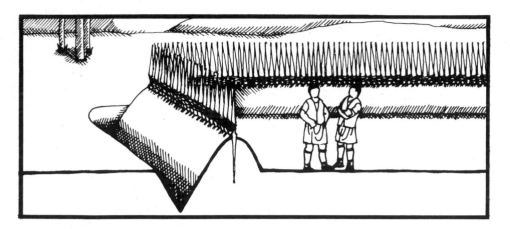

4. Part of the defences of a marching camp as they may have looked, with outer defensive ditch and earth bank. The top of the bank is defended by pointed stakes tied together.

Right 6. Aerial view of the Roman marching camp on Malham Moor (North Yorkshire), identified from the air in the 1950s. Situated at a height of 1,250 feet above sea level, it measures 1,020 × 865 feet, and has four entrances (arrowed) protected by internal *claviculae* (see ill. 9).

First of all, though, we must say what a fort is not. It is not a camp, even though the two terms are frequently confused. A camp is not designed for permanent occupation: often it was constructed to protect the bivouac of a single night's duration. It had been the practice of the Roman army, from at least the third century BC to build an earthwork, topped by a timber palisade and fronted by a V-shaped ditch, every time it stopped for the night. The defences were generally slight, 5 to 10 feet wide and no more than 6 feet high, and follow the dictates of the terrain rather than a strictly rectangular layout. Within, the soldiers pitched their tents in orderly lines. Nearly 350 of these marching camps are now known in Britain, largely from aerial reconnaissance, and the constant discovery of fresh camps, especially in Scotland, is helping to illuminate in some detail the progressive advance of the Roman army.

Occasionally marching camps have more massive defences, such as the fine example on the Stainmore Pass at Rey Cross*: here the ramparts are twenty feet wide and may have been so constructed because the ditch was left partly undug due to underlying bedrock. Normally substantial earthworks of this kind imply a longer period of occupation, sometimes marked by gravelled roads, pits and gullies in the interior. But these are not forts either: if accommodation was provided by tents rather than by barracks, the earthwork is a 'camp'. The so-called labour camps are of this kind, built to shelter a unit engaged on building a nearby fortlet, fort or even frontier barrier, jobs which might take months or even years to complete.[6] The tiny practice camps on the other hand never even held tented accommodation: they were the work of army gangs who were being trained in ditch digging and rampart building.[7]

5. A Roman tent designed for a tent-unit (*contubernium*) of eight men, based on information from classical sources and surviving scraps of leather tents.

Right 7, 8. Plans of marching camps at Raedykes*(1), Dalginross (2) and Swine Hill*(3) and of practice camps at Bootham Stray (1), Doldinnas*(2) and Loughor*(3). Note the difference in scale. For the entrance types see ill. 9.

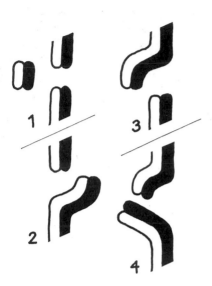

9. Entrances to marching camps, four different types: the *clavicula*, a curved extension of rampart and ditch, usually inside the area of the camp (2), more rarely external (3); the *titulum*, a short, straight piece of rampart and ditch covering the entrance on the outside of the camp (1); and the 'Stracathro' type, a combination of external *clavicula* and a straight oblique extension of rampart and ditch, used only by one of Agricola's camp builders in the 80s AD in Scotland (4).

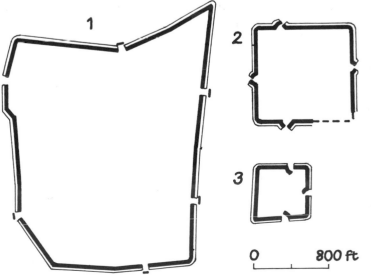

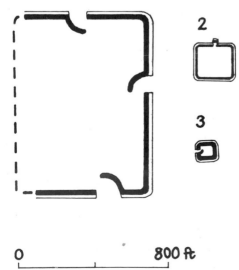

10. The Roman fort at Birdoswald on Hadrian's Wall as it may have appeared about AD 130, after the rebuilding of the Wall in this sector (far left) in stone. The earthworks of the Vallum are visible in the foreground. This fort was designed to take a regiment of 1,000 and is therefore larger and has more barrack accommodation than our imaginary fort. At Birdoswald much of the circuit of walls survives today in impressive fashion (see ill. 52), but little of the interior has been investigated.

11. The earth ramparts of an Iron Age hill fort were about 15 feet high and fronted by a ditch 20 feet deep.

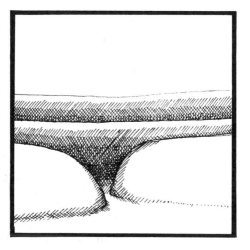

12. A Roman fort gateway. The top of the towers was about 24 feet high, the top of the parapet about 17 feet.

Our imaginary Roman fort is a very different structure from any of the camps just mentioned. It is a permanent base for the five hundred soldiers stationed there, who live in barracks, not under leather. It is situated in a fine position, on a flat spur above a river, and controlling the approaches to an important mountain pass. Water is readily available from the river, and the road which joins the fort with neighbouring forts a day's march away to the north and the south provides a very necessary communications link and supplies line. The fort does not present dauntingly massive defences: it appears puny besides the gigantic earthworks of a prehistoric Iron Age hill fort, or the lofty stone walls of the later medieval castle. But then the military thinking which lay behind its conception was very different from the defensive strategy of an earlier and of a later age. It was not designed as an impregnable stronghold, as its garrison is trained to charge out from the gateways and meet its adversary at close quarters on open ground. Nevertheless its two V-shaped defensive ditches (not intended to be water-filled like a medieval moat) are obstacles deep enough to deter all but the most determined attacker, and the rampart which lies beyond is substantial enough to withstand assault in an emergency. It consists of a stone wall 5 feet wide and 12 feet high, with a crenellated top protecting the patrol walk behind. Backing the stone wall is a sloping bank of earth.

14, 15. The defences of the first fort on this spot (above) had a rampart entirely of earth, held in place by cut turves front and back, and surmounted by a patrol-walk of timber. At a later period (below) the earth bank was cut back and a vertical stone wall inserted in front of it. Some extra soil has altered the profile of the remaining portion of the earth bank.

13. The gate towers of a medieval castle, some 40–50 feet high.

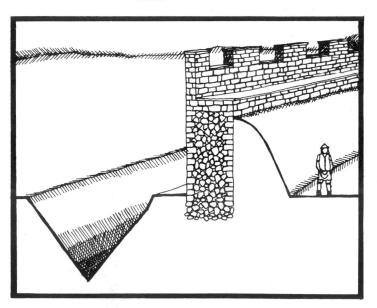

The basic layout of the fort has not changed. It takes the shape of a shortened playing card, squarish with rounded corners. The curtain wall is broken by just four gateways, one in each side. The gates are impressive structures, each with two carriageways closed by stout wooden doors, a guard-chamber on each side to control admission, surmounted by towers above which provide look-out points at a higher level than those of the patrol-walk. There are further look-out posts, turrets, at each corner, and another between the corners and each gateway.

The neat regularity of the exterior of the fort is reflected by the tight, orderly, rational disposition of the interior buildings: its planning spells efficiency and discipline. Broad gravelled roads throughout give ease of access to both men and supplies. A road runs close to the back of the defences all the way round the fort (*via sagularis*); another joins the gates on the short axis of the fort (*via principalis*); a third links the headquarters building with the front gate (*via praetoria*); and the fourth main road runs from the rear of the headquarters down to the back gate (*via decumana*). The road along the short axis behind the central range of buildings, not linking gateways, is the *via quintana*.

16. A fort gateway, with twin passageways and rampart walk above. The towers on either side have a guard chamber on the ground floor, a first floor on a level with the rampart walk, and a flat open top for observation from a higher level. The rectangular panel above the arches carries an inscription giving the name of the emperor, the year of his reign, in which the fort was built, and the name of the regiment which erected it.

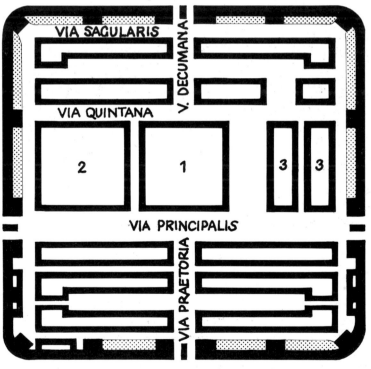

17. Typical fort layout with division into three parts: a central range with HQ (1), the commandant's house (2) and granaries (3); and a front portion (*praetentura* bottom third) and the rear portion (*retentura*) with barracks, stores and other buildings.

18. Inside the *principia* with its paved courtyard and well (bottom left) flanking colonnades, and a hall beyond lit by the clerestory windows above.

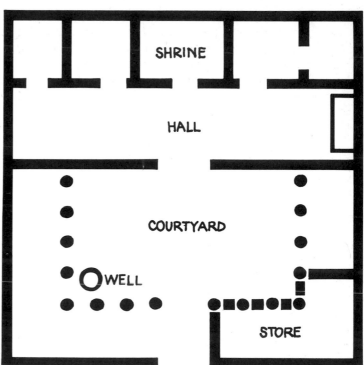

19. Plan of a typical headquarters building. The platform at the right hand end of the hall is the dais for the commanding officer, and part of the courtyard colonnade has been blocked up to provide extra storage space, especially for weapons.

At the centre of the fort is the headquarters building, the *principia*. This is the hub of the fort's activities: the place where commands are given, notices posted, pay distributed and punishment decided; the place where the unit assembles to hear an address from the commanding officer; the focus, too, of loyalty to the Emperor. It consists of three parts: a paved courtyard, with a well in one corner, flanked by colonnades on three sides (part of it blocked off to provide extra room for stores); a cross-hall running the full width of the building, with a platform at the right-hand end where the commandant stands when he addresses his men (*tribunal*); and beyond a row of five rooms at the back of the building. The central room is the shrine (*aedes*), guarded by sentries. It contains a statue of the Emperor, and the standards of the unit's centuries as well; the regimental pay chest lies below a trap-door in the floor. On either side are the rooms for administration: for the adjutant and his clerks on one side, responsible for the smooth running of the day-to-day rotas and the ordering and distribution of supplies, the other pair of rooms for the standard-bearers of each century who look after the pay and savings of the troops. All the details of the unit's individual members are on file here.

21. Plan of a typical commandant's house. The entrance from the *via principalis* is at the bottom.

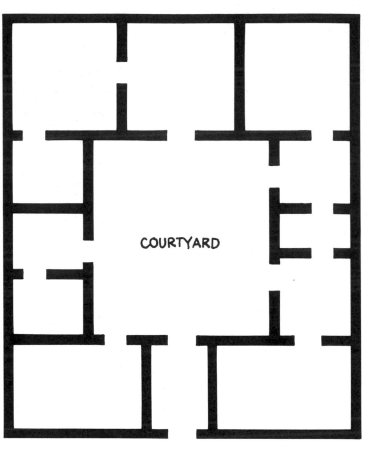

COURTYARD

20. View inside a typical commandant's house with gravelled court and entrance from the *via principalis* to the right.

Adjacent to the headquarters building is the residence of the commanding officer and his family, the *praetorium*. Like the HQ it is a substantial stone-built structure with a slate roof. It is constructed on the principle of a Mediterranean courtyard house, however unsuitable this might seem in northern climes, and has its rooms ranged round all four sides of a central, draughty court-yard. One room is the family's private dining room, another is reserved for receiving official visitors. A degree of comfort is provided by a couple of rooms with under-floor heating, and of hygiene by a private toilet, but there is no set of baths. For that the CO needed to join his men at the garrison bath-house beyond the fort walls.

22, 23, 24. A typical fort granary as it may have appeared (below) and in plan (far right). The photograph (right) shows part of the granary floor supports in the fort at Housesteads on Hadrian's Wall (see also ill. 65).

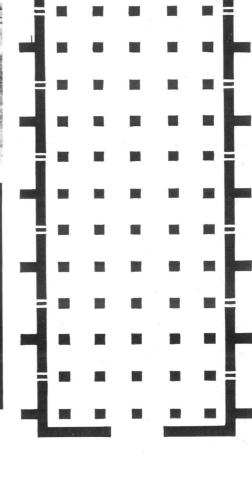

On the other side of the headquarters building is a pair of granaries where the garrison's foodstuffs are stored (*horrea*). Each is a long rectangular building with buttresses all round and a heavy tiled roof. The buttresses are provided to take the weight of the sturdy roof-beams and of the tiles above: a watertight roof is essential in a building of this kind. But ventilation is equally crucial, so wooden louvers are placed between the buttresses just below roof level to give plenty of air to the inside, and the floor of the building is raised and ventilated to keep the contents free from damp. Of the contents grain is the most important commodity, stored partly in wooden bins, partly in sacks on either side of the central gangway; and the other staple ingredients of the soldiers' diet including vegetables, cheese, meat, wine and oil, are stored here, on hooks and racks in the upper part of each granary. There is also a rectangular loading platform, covered by a portico to make sure supplies do not get wet during off-loading, at one end of each granary.

25, 26. Plan of a typical barrack (top) and a reconstruction sketch of part of it (below), showing the wider centurion's quarters at one end. The bottom two and a half feet of the outer wall are built of stone – above is a timber framework with wattle and daub panels between.

These buildings, the headquarters, the commandant's house and the granaries, occupy the central third of the fort's interior; the rest of it, both the front part (*praetentura*) on the other side of the *via principalis*, and the back portion behind the central range (*retentura*), are occupied by barrack blocks to house the infantry soldiers. There are six in all, each holding a century of eighty men. These are not substantial stone buildings like the central range: they have timber superstructures resting on stone footings, and the internal partitions are wooden too. The barrack is L-shaped, with more spacious accommodation for the centurion and his second-in-command (*optio*) at one end. The rest of the block has ten compartments facing onto a verandah, and each compartment is further subdivided into a front and a back room. Eight men share each of these compartments, keeping their weapons, equipment and personal belongings in the outer room, and sleeping on mattresses in the inner room. Much of the soldier's time when not outside the fort walls is spent here, cleaning armour, relaxing, eating. There is no communal dining room anywhere in the fort, so meals are cooked in ovens near the back of the rampart and eaten in the barracks. But the barracks are not particularly comfortable, and there is no heating except for the occasional portable brazier.

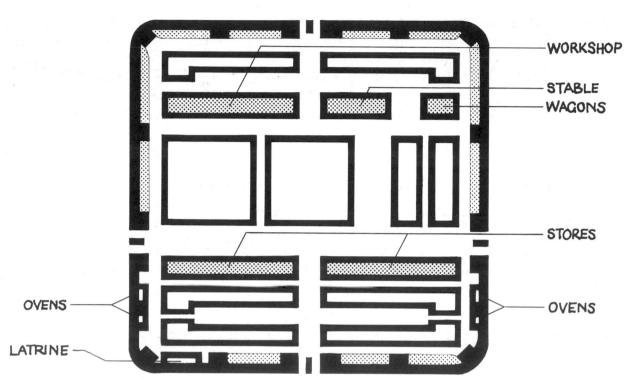

WORKSHOP

STABLE

WAGONS

STORES

OVENS — — OVENS

LATRINE

28. The latrine at Housesteads, at the southeast corner of the fort (8 on ill. 49). The soldiers sat on wooden seats erected over the deep sewers on either side of the central floor area. They washed their sponges in the water which ran in the channel in front of them, and rinsed their hands in the two basins in the centre.

The other buildings inside the fort include a workshop, where armour can be mended and leather repaired; stores for bulky equipment too large to keep in the barracks; a stable block for pack-animals and the horses used by despatch riders and officers. There is no hospital, and soldiers who fall sick are taken to a larger fort nearby, which does have medical facilities. Close to the rampart is the fort latrine with standards of hygiene unparalleled until the twentieth century: timber seats have been erected over stone-built, flushed sewers; and sponges, the Roman equivalent of toilet paper, are rinsed in the running water carried in the gutter in front of each seat. There are also tubs of water to wash the hands before leaving. There are other water tanks placed around the defensive wall to catch rainwater for drinking and washing; but for proper ablutions the soldier is glad to escape outside the walls of the fort to the comfort and warmth of the garrison bath-house.

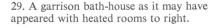

30. Plan of a typical bath-house showing changing room (*apodyterium*, 1), cold room (*frigidarium*, 2), cold water bath (3), warm room (*tepidarium*, 4), hot dry room (*sudatorium*, 5), hot moist room (*caldarium*, 6), hot water baths (7) and furnaces (8).

29. A garrison bath-house as it may have appeared with heated rooms to right.

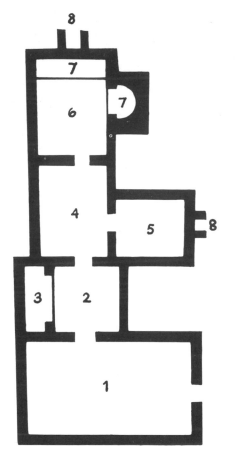

The bath-house is the most substantial structure outside the defences: it is also an essential requirement for both the relaxation and the health of every Roman soldier. Here the off-duty soldier passes through a series of rooms of different temperatures, first cool, then warm, then hot. Sweating profusely in the hot, steamy room (*caldarium*) he scrapes himself down with a blunt metal instrument (*strigil*) to remove the dirt from the pores (soap was almost unknown in antiquity). He then takes a splash in the hot plunge-bath and follows the rooms back to the changing room. A dip in the cold plunge-bath helps to close the pores and prevent him catching cold.

The bath-house stands out from the motley collection of timber shacks forming the shanty town of a civilian village which sprawls around the fort walls. A garrison of five hundred men serves as a magnet for merchants and tradesmen seeking a ready market for their wares. The taverns, brothels and gambling dens also have a fail-safe attraction for off-duty soldiers with money to spend and hours to while away. Some soldiers have common-law wives and families living in the relative squalor of the village, but they are not allowed to marry until they have retired from active service (only in the third century was this to change). There are also the families of retired auxiliaries here, men who prefer to stay with their former comrades and till a nearby plot of land or practise a craft rather than seek their fortune away from the military zone. Beyond, on the horizon, the artificially levelled parade ground is a reminder to them of their past life, and the tombstones of the garrison cemetery are a reminder, too, of what is to come.

We must not think from the generalized description above that every fort looked like this, or that fort design remained standardized throughout the three and a half centuries of Roman occupation in Britain. The regularity of the fort just imagined became only normal towards the end of the first century, and the building or rebuilding of its defences and central buildings in stone only gradually became commonplace in the province during the course of the second century. Similarly our fort was designed for the simplest type of auxiliary force, the infantry unit 500 strong, but from the late first century there were five other types of auxiliary regiment in Britain, and the interior buildings of the fort varied to meet their respective needs. There are, furthermore, many details of construction, especially of superstructures, about which we are ignorant, and these problems have been glossed over in the account above. So we must repeat, there is no such thing as a typical Roman fort. But the above description may serve as a yard-stick by which to measure the actual examples of Roman forts in Britain, both the earth and timber forts of the first century, the relatively standardized examples of the second which come nearest to our imaginary fort, and the very fundamental changes of the late Empire. Fort building and design were ever the subject of experimentation and change, and this slow process of evolution will be outlined in the remaining chapters.

2 The First Century

31. The ditch system at Hod Hill, with rampart (1), V-ditches (2, 3) and outer 'Punic' ditch (4).

Forts of the mid-first century

In AD 43 four Roman legions and a large number of auxiliaries landed in Kent under the command of Aulus Plautius and soon pushed westwards to the Thames. A pause followed to allow the next stage of the advance, as far as Colchester, the most powerful British stronghold, to be completed in the company of the emperor Claudius himself. With the fall of Colchester the invading force split up into three divisions and fanned out to conquer the rest of the country. In the wake of subjugation came carefully planned military control, in the form of forts, fortresses, roads and supply-bases. Some details have begun to emerge in the last few years of these early campaign strongholds, notably at Colchester where something is now known of the 48-acre legionary fortress built in the winter of 43–4; but many of these military sites of the conquest period lie buried beneath later towns, and our knowledge of them is at best fragmentary.

The legion chosen to spearhead the advance to the south-west from 44 onwards was the Second Augusta, then commanded by the young Vespasian, who, twenty-five years later, was to become emperor. His biographer Suetonius informs us that he fought thirty battles, and overcame two powerful tribes and more than twenty hill forts. One of these was Hod Hill* in Dorset, where a heavy bombardment of artillery fire on the chieftain's hut-group was apparently intimidating enough to secure surrender. The north-west corner of the hill fort was then used, in a highly unusual departure from normal Roman practice, as the site of a Roman garrison fort, occupied for just six or seven years, from 44 to 51/2. The existing, massive hill fort ramparts formed its north and west sides, and new, much slighter, Roman defences were built on the south and east. Like all fort-defences in Britain until the end of the first century, these used not a scrap of stonework: here at Hod a core of packed chalk was faced back and front with turf, and topped by a wooden breastwork and patrol walk. We should envisage an overall height of perhaps 10 to 15 feet, a substantial but not impregnable barrier. A complicated ditch-system afforded further protection. The outermost ditch, 5 feet deep, had a near-vertical outer edge and a gently sloping inner edge: this is what Roman military writers call a 'Punic' ditch. Then came a flat area 55 feet wide separating it from the two inner ditches, also 5 feet deep but with a

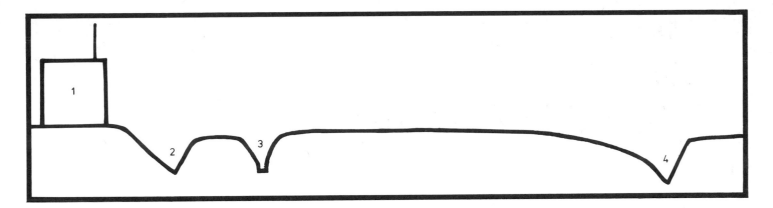

normal V-profile. A further ditch was added for good measure at the vulnerable south-east corner. The Roman military thinking behind this system was along the following lines. The attacker meets his first obstacle 90 feet away from the fort, which is about the killing range of a missile projected from the ramparts. He then easily negotiates the outer ditch with its alluring gentle profile, but finds the going tougher when he reaches the V-profile of the inner ditches. If he then loses heart and turns to flee, the very steep outer profile of the outer ditch comes as a nasty surprise: to the Romans, 'Punic' was synonymous with 'treacherous'. This system of defence might look fine on paper, but it was presumably found unnecessary or ineffective in the field: Hod Hill enshrines an example of military theory which never became widespread practice.[1] Similar thinking can be seen behind the wedge shape of the causeways at the south and east gates, designed to cause maximum confusion for a hypothetical horde of attackers, who would jostle one another as the space became more restricted the nearer they approached the gateways.[2]

Within the 10 acres enclosed by the defences at Hod Hill were a number of timber buildings, and the outline plan of these, reconstructed by the judicious trenching of Sir Ian Richmond during the 1950s, provides the earliest example of a Roman fort-plan in Britain, and our only complete illustration in the province of a garrison-post of the Claudian conquest-period. The fort, however, was not designed to take a single auxiliary cohort as was the later standard practice: military equipment appropriate to both legionaries and auxiliaries, ploughed up here over the centuries, suggested before digging commenced that both were brigaded together within the same defences. Its layout, therefore, makes allowances for the joint force, and there are in fact some buildings which we cannot at present identify for certain.

Before we have a look at these, however, a word or two must be said about how the plan of timber structures can be so confidently deduced: the wood itself, except in a few cases of timber strapping used to strengthen earth ramparts, has long since vanished, often because it was taken away by demolition gangs on the withdrawal of the garrison. Rather the plans can be identified by excavating the post-pits and foundation-trenches which were cut in the natural rock or subsoil (at Hod Hill chalk) to receive the timber-framed superstructures. For gateways a separate pit is dug for each upright, and when the timber has been raised by a derrick or crane to its vertical position, the post-pit is packed around it with back-filled soil, cobbles or stones. This method of post-hole construction is sometimes used also for some or all of the interior buildings, although the individual post-pits are of course much smaller. But it was generally more convenient to dig a foundation-slot outlining the plan of the building to be erected, and then placing the uprights of the timber framing at intervals along it before backfilling and packing the slot. The problems really begin only when we try to envisage the superstructure. The panels between the timber framing were probably normally filled by sections of wattle-interlace covered with daub and finished off (at least on the inside) with a plaster wash: we often know this from the remains of burnt daub left behind by the demolition squad on withdrawal. But some buildings, especially the granaries where weather-proofing was so essential, would certainly have received the stouter construction of timber planking; indeed some forts where archaeological evidence for daub is entirely missing may have been completely constructed in this way, but this was probably unusual.

32. Aerial photograph of the Roman fort at Hod Hill, Dorset, showing the Iron Age hill-fort defences (right) and the added Roman defences on the south and east (left). The plan of some of the interior buildings, and especially the T-shaped roadway, show clearly as parched lines in the ripening crop.

The buildings at Hod Hill are arranged about a T-shaped roadway. This layout, with the *via principalis* on the long rather than the short axis and with no rear portion (*retentura*), is paralleled in contemporary forts on the continent but went out of fashion in the second half of the first century. The simple headquarters building (*principia* **1**) lies at the junction of the T: it has a courtyard and three administrative rooms at the back. The barrack blocks are also clearly recognizable, with a more spacious officers' quarters at one end, and some were presumably designed for the legionary infantry, some for auxiliary cavalrymen **5**.[3] The undivided cells of the ordinary soldiers (*contubernia*) suggest rather more cramped conditions than was later the norm. The three courtyard buildings around the HQ pose greater problems of identification: Richmond thought that the one behind **2** was for the commander of the legionary contingent, and that the two facing it were, respectively, the auxiliary commandant's house **3** and the hospital **4**; but this is very far from certain, and other interpretations are possible.[4] There was just a single granary, conveniently situated near the east gate **6**: its plan is easily recognizable, by the neat rectangular grid of posts which supported the raised floor to keep its contents free of damp and vermin. The latrines **7** were near the south gate, and stables **8** in the north-west corner.

Hod Hill gives us an excellent idea of a garrison post in the early years of the conquest which is in striking contrast to the fully-evolved layout exemplified at Fendoch forty years later. Another remarkable illustration of these early years is the site at Longthorpe, discovered from the air in 1961 and partly excavated between 1967 and 1973. Longthorpe is not a fort, nor is it a full legionary fortress either which would normally have covered some 50 acres. It belongs to a class of fortifications, completely unsuspected until the last twenty years or so, which have become known as vexillation fortresses. Twelve have now been identified[5], most of them between 20 and 30 acres, and thus intermediate in size between fort and fortress. The evidence of military equipment from Longthorpe suggests, as at Hod Hill, that legionaries and auxiliaries were brigaded together in battle units, and these vexillation fortresses served as stores-bases and winter quarters during the campaigns.

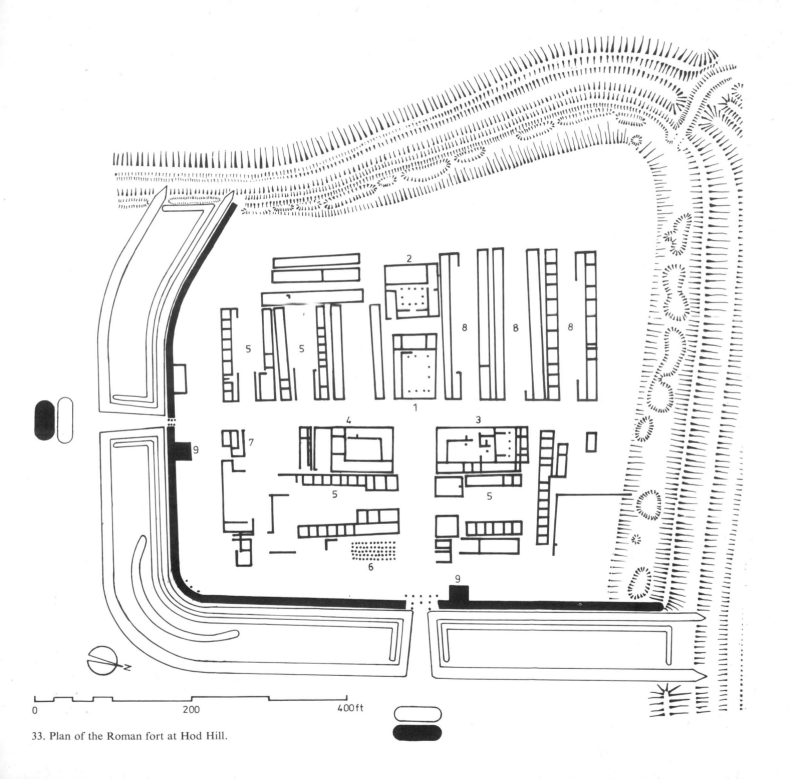

33. Plan of the Roman fort at Hod Hill.

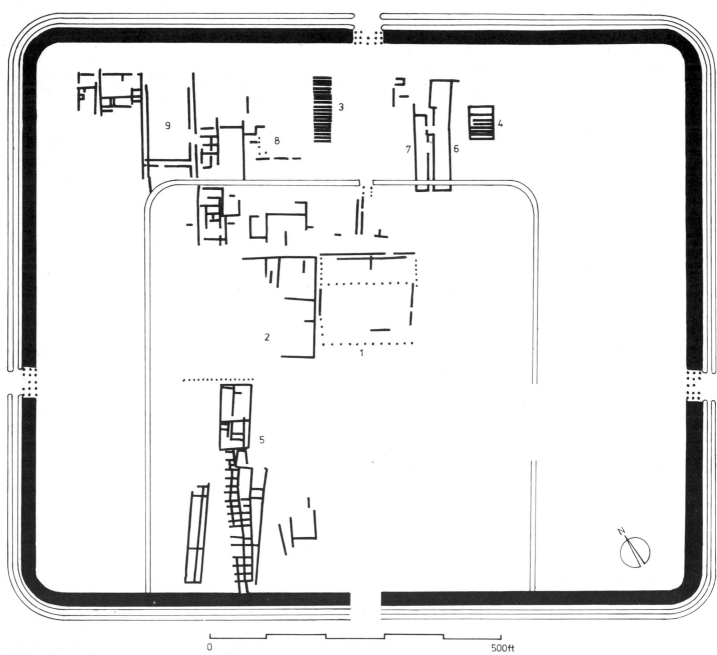

34. Plan of the earth-and-timber vexillation
fortress at Longthorpe with *principia* (1),
commandant's house (?) (2), granary (3),
additional store-house (4), legionary barrack
(5), auxiliary barrack (6), stable (?) (7),
courtyard building (?) (8), and wagon-park
(?) (9). The rampart accompanying the ditch
of the reduced fort is not shown. The site
now lies below a golf-course.

0   500ft

At Longthorpe the defences are regular enough: the rampart and two defensive ditches enclose a rectangle of 27 acres, and the two excavated gates (and probably all four) had double carriageways and flanking towers. But the timber buildings traced within this circuit were often hard to identify. The granary by the north gate **3** and another store building further east **4** were conventional enough, but of the other structures which yielded a more or less coherent plan the headquarters building **1** and a legionary barrack block **5** call for special comment. The *principia* had a portico at the front and a cobbled yard before the main courtyard area. Beyond it was a large hall, possibly subdivided, but at the rear of that there was perhaps a corridor but none of the normal office rooms expected in such buildings. The barrack block is extraordinary. Not only is its ill-aligned layout most striking, but the men's quarters seem to have had a partitioned verandah in front of the normal pair of rooms and an extra lean-to behind. There were 14 *contubernia* in all, and an excessively spacious centurion's quarters: in fact this Longthorpe barrack is the longest yet discovered (343 feet) in the Roman Empire.

The garrison at Longthorpe, when at full strength, was perhaps about 2,800 in all, of which about 1,000 were auxiliaries, the rest legionaries. The scanty finds suggest a longer occupation than Hod Hill, probably about 15 years (*c.* AD 45–61). But if haste, or at least lack of care, is shown in the irregular nature of the original plan, haste is even more obvious towards the end of the fortress' life. Inside the main fortifications is another rampart and a single ditch enclosing 11 acres. This is not a marching camp but a reduced fort, because it too has a proper timber gateway and tower at the north entrance. Yet there are no secondary timber buildings within which can be associated with the new defences: the standing structures there were apparently left unaltered. How can this be explained? In AD 60 or 61 Queen Boudicca of the Iceni led her famous revolt against Roman rule and sacked the towns of Colchester (founded when the legionary fortress there was dismantled in 49), London and St Albans. We know from Tacitus that part of a legion under Petillius Cerealis was cut to pieces before Suetonius Paulinus, the governor, had time to march back from Wales and crush the rebellion. Both the dating evidence and the geographical position suggest that Longthorpe was Cerealis' base, and the inner ditch and rampart look very much like the panic defences for his depleted forces after the disaster inflicted by Boudicca.

Whether Longthorpe and Hod Hill are typical of Claudian forts in Britain remains to be seen, but work at a third, Waddon Hill in Dorset, has uncovered another puzzling set of structures. We cannot explain away these irregularities by saying that the Roman military high-command's thinking about forts at this time was in a state of flux, for perfectly good examples of well planned, carefully constructed forts of the same period are known on the continent. It is probably best, therefore, to regard our examples in Britain as semi-permanent holding bases, not temporary camps, but not forts designed to be permanent either. A year or two's occupation only may have been envisaged at the outset, and the care expended on the buildings of a permanent fort is therefore missing. That Longthorpe was occupied for as long as fifteen years might hint that the Roman advance in Britain was not as swift as had been hoped: Caesar had, after all, taken only nine years to subdue the whole of Gaul.

A decade later the realities of the military situation in Britain had been accepted. The base founded at Exeter in the mid 50s, for example, a small legionary fortress covering just 38 acres, shows no hint of the irregularities discovered at Longthorpe; and the very impressive stone bath-house, with the largest set of heated rooms yet found in Britain, indicates a degree of permanence absent in the planners' minds at Longthorpe or Hod. The same impression comes from the 48-acre legionary fortress founded also in the mid-50s at Usk in South Wales. Parts of this site, largely unencumbered by later building unlike Exeter, have been excavated in recent years, and a clear picture of a carefully planned regular layout has been obtained. The *via principalis*, lined with a stone-built drain, was flanked by imposing timber colonnades, and parts of a stores-compound or workshop and of a tribune's house, as well as several granaries, have also been found.[6]

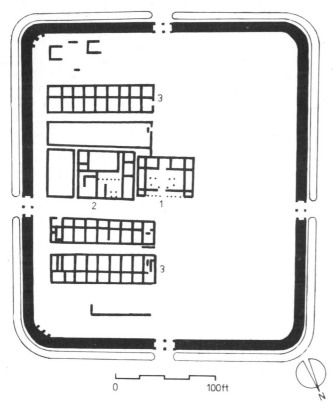

35. Plan of the small fort at Nanstallon near
Bodmin, *c.* AD 60, with *principia* (1),
commandant's house (2), and barracks (3).
The timber gates had twin passageways and
towers above, but no guardrooms. The
western half is unexcavated. There is nothing
to see at the site now.

commandant's house **2** has a cramped internal court but a
generous reception or dining-room at the rear, and a yard
to the east,[7] and the barracks are also small, in keeping
with the scaled-down proportions of the fort. They have
no verandah, nor is there the usual wider block at the end
for officers, although the arrangement of the internal
partitions suggests these lay at the east end. The type
of garrison at Nanstallon is uncertain, as only half of it
has been dug, but its tiny size must mean several detachments of the regiment were outposted in fortlets, like the
contemporary one at Martinhoe* in north Devon designed
for a *centuria* of 80 men.

The trauma of Boudicca's rebellion was not easily
forgotten. It had been touch and go as to whether Rome
would lose the whole province; and even after the rebels
had been crushed Nero's advisers may have seriously
contemplated a total Roman pull-out. Caution was the
keynote of the next decade (61–71), and there were
increased troop concentrations in east Anglia and the
Midlands. One of the new foundations in about 61 was
the fort called the Lunt at Baginton* near Coventry. The
earliest structures here appear to belong to a large fort or
store base the precise size of which is unknown. A couple
of years or so after its foundation it was equipped with a
circular stockade, a stout wooden fence about nine feet
high enclosing an 'arena' a hundred Roman feet in
diameter **2**. In the absence of parallels its purpose is
uncertain, but the hypothesis that it is a *gyrus* or training-
ground for horses and cavalry recruits seems convincing.
Then in about 64 new defences were built to enclose about
3 acres, and the eastern defences, instead of being straight
made an odd detour to avoid the existing *gyrus*.[8] Such
a sinuous course is unparalleled in British forts and is
very rare on the continent. The entire area within this
reduced fort has been stripped and its building-plans
revealed. Some are quite conventional. The *principia*, for
example **1**, has a large courtyard flanked by long rooms,
exactly as at Nanstallon, and there are three (rather than
five) rooms at the rear, the middle one with a sunken pit
for pay and valuables.[9] The granaries too **3,4** are normal.
The barracks **5** are different from Nanstallon's but not
like the evolved examples of the Flavian period either:
they have a verandah, but no projecting area for officers
and no subdivisions in each *contubernium*. We can be less

Bases such as Exeter and Usk did not stand alone:
they were the hub of an often elaborate network of smaller
forts and fortlets, but few are known in detail from the
50s or 60s. One of the few is Nanstallon, deep down in
the Cornish peninsula, a tiny 2-acre post founded in the
late 50s and garrisoned for about twenty years. The
principia **1** is unusual in having a recessed portico and its
long axis parallel to the *via principalis* rather than at
right-angles to it, but in other respects this is an embryonic
version of the fully-fledged auxiliary fort headquarters
buildings that were to appear two decades later. The

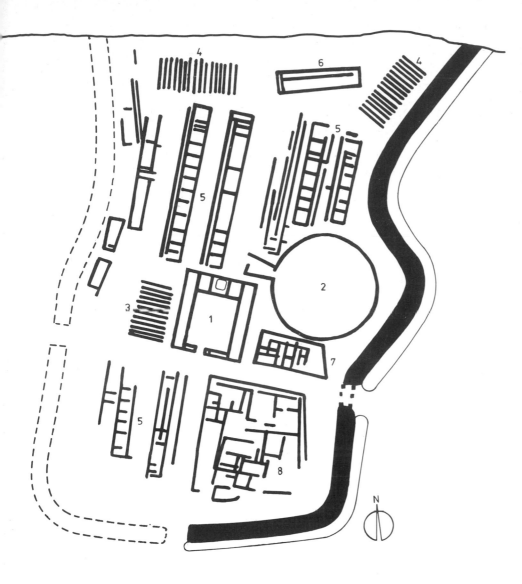

36. Plan of the earth-and-timber fort (and training centre?) at the Lunt, Baginton, in its later second phase (*c.* AD 70), with *principia* (1), *gyrus* (2), granaries (3, 4), barracks (5), stables (6) and two buildings of uncertain purpose (7, 8). The northern edge of the site is now eroded, and the course of the western defences conjectural. Buildings 2 and 3, together with the east gate and part of the east defences, have been reconstructed, and the plans of 1 and of the structures in the NE corner (4, 5, 6) have been laid out in concrete.

certain about some of the other buildings. The one marked **8**, has, for example, been interpreted as the commandant's house (*praetorium*). But this is an exceptionally large building occupying the whole south-east quarter of the fort, and such a generous allocation of space to the commandant of a small post seems hard to justify. The Lunt, however, is not a typical fort at all—the *gyrus* alone testifies to that—and is perhaps best regarded as a special army training-school.[10]

The Lunt, then, appears to add a new aspect to our knowledge of Roman army organization in the first century; but it is also of great importance for the attempts that have been made there to understand its structures not just as two-dimensional ground-plans but in elevation as well. Brian Hobley, who carried out most of this work,[11] prefers to call the attempts simulations rather than reconstructions, for inevitably there are many details of the superstructure about which we know little or nothing.

37. Photograph of the granary at the Lunt, Baginton, reconstructed by Royal Engineers of the British Army in 1973. Wagons could be wheeled up to the loading platforms at either end to facilitate off-loading of supplies.

The only certain fact about the granary, for example, is that it was erected on 105 posts set at 5 foot intervals: the height of the building, the pitch of the roof, the position and number of the louvers and the precise nature and appearance of the wall-finish, are all conjecture. It is, however, unlikely that the Roman granary which stood on this spot looked significantly different. Similarly the superstructure of the re-erected east gateway is not certain, but not pure guesswork either: it is based on examples depicted in sculptured form on Trajan's column

in Rome. For the ramparts on either side, which have an earth core faced back and front with cut turves, some of the instructions in Roman military handbooks were followed, although the turf blocks were cut larger than recommended to prevent bulging. Excavation showed that the rampart was about 18 feet wide at base and stood on a gravelled foundation, and in the simulation it was found that a 65° angle of batter gives reasonable stability and allows for a 6-foot wide walkway 12 feet above the ground. The Lunt today, therefore, probably provides a

38. Photograph of the east gateway at the Lunt, Baginton, reconstructed in three days in 1970 using prefabricated timbers. The granary is visible through the open gate, and a timber breastwork shields the patrol-walk on either side.

fairly accurate idea of what earth-and-timber forts looked like in first-century Roman Britain, even though there was a good deal of variation in the materials and type of construction used. But the dangers of assuming too much from too little have been highlighted by a recent discovery at Chester. There the fortress rampart built in the 70s had, as at the Lunt, a front and rear facing of turf, and a core (of rubble) stabilized by two courses of horizontal timber 'strapping'. The surprise was that at Chester it actually survived to wall-walk height, which, even allowing for decomposition and compression over 1,900 years, suggests that it was only 7 feet high to this level. What is more, the rampart walk was not of timber but of sandstone paving slabs. If Chester was normal, then the defences today at the Lunt are misleadingly high; but there is no way of telling if Chester *was* normal. Simulation work stimulates lots of questions, but it does not necessarily provide all the right answers.

The sagging and slipping of the Lunt ramparts in the ten years they have been standing shows how important a factor stability is. This was most commonly provided by timber strapping at intervals throughout the core, as at Chester, but occasionally both the front and the back of the rampart were revetted in timber instead of turf. Such 'box ramparts', widely known on the continent, have only been found in Britain on a handful of sites, all built around AD 60.[12] More common is the provision of timber-work at the front only, especially in forts built rather later in the first century, and it is likely that the evidence for this in many more examples was removed when the front of the rampart was cut back and a stone wall inserted in the second century.

There was plenty of variety too in the ditch systems. The Hod Hill complex was rare, probably because artillery machines were mounted on special platforms at the back of the rampart.[13] But normal auxiliary units did not have artillery until at least the second century, and simpler V-shaped ditches were the norm, usually in pairs.[14] Flat-bottomed ditches are most uncommon and are normally found only where, as at Usk, the natural soil was too loose to permit the V-profile.

The late first century: army changes

In the autumn of 69, after Italy had been rent by a year of fierce fighting and three successive emperors had been proclaimed and toppled, Vespasian established himself as sole master of the Roman world. The Flavian period which thus began (and lasted until 96)[15] saw many changes, both in the composition of the army and in the military situation in Britain. It was in the 70s for example that the 500-strong auxiliary regiments were first supplemented by new ones 1,000-strong (milliary). As with some of the 500-strong units we are ignorant of certain details in the composition of these new forces. The infantry cohort (*cohors peditata milliaria*) had ten centuries, presumably each of 80 men, and a total strength of 800: '1,000-strong' is just a convenient, not an accurate, label. The cavalry wing (*ala milliaria*) may have fallen even shorter of the thousand mark, for we know it had 24 *turmae* (compared with sixteen in a 500-strong counterpart), which means a paper strength of only 720 (plus officers) if each *turma* comprised 30 men.[16] With the part-mounted milliary cohort (*cohors peditata milliaria*) there is the same numbers problem as with its 500-strong counterpart: we know it had ten infantry centuries and eight cavalry troops, and if each century had 60 rather than 80 men (p 7) the strength was 840 plus officers.[17] All three types appear in Britain, but the *ala milliaria* was limited to one a province.[18] Another change in the 80s was in the composition of the First Cohort of every legion; six centuries of 80 men became five centuries of 160 men.

Vespasian knew at first hand the qualities needed for a military commander in Britain, and he was responsible for sending to the province three outstanding governors who pursued a policy of total conquest with astonishing speed and ruthless efficiency. Petillius Cerealis (71–4), former commander of the Ninth (p 27), undertook the subjugation of the Brigantes tribe of northern England who had given repeated trouble from the early 50s. Julius Frontinus (74–8) completed the pacification of Wales and was the architect of the permanent network of roads and garrison forts there, including the legionary fortresses at Caerleon and Chester.[19]

The finishing touches at Chester, and the final mopping-up of the Ordovices tribe of north Wales, were carried out by Frontinus' successor Gnaeus Julius Agricola, the most celebrated of the governors of Roman Britain (78–84/5). Some of the adulation in the biography of him written by his son-in-law Tacitus can be seen as stock literary cliché, some as due to the partisanship of its author; yet the very real magnitude of Agricola's achievement is a fact confirmed by archaeology and aerial photography. In just seven years—longer, it is true, than the span allotted to most governors—he completed the pacification of Wales, he consolidated Cerealis' conquests as far as the Tyne-Solway line, and he pushed Roman arms into southern Scotland and thence up the eastern plains to the mouth of the river Spey. The area he covered was almost as vast as that subjugated during the preceding thirty-five years. This was more than mere military showmanship: conquest was accompanied by immediate consolidation with a network of forts and roads. Over fifty new forts are known to have been constructed during his governorship, as well as the legionary fortress at Inchtuthil (Perthshire) and possibly that at York. The achievement is staggering, in terms both of military strategy and of the organizational skills of the Roman army.

The culmination of the Scottish campaigns was the battle of Mons Graupius in 84, possibly in the region of Mount Bennachie (20 miles north-west of Aberdeen) where a marching camp of 144 acres, larger than any other in north Scotland, was discovered in 1975.[20] Ten thousand Caledonians under the leadership of Calgacus were killed, with the reported loss of only 360 on the Roman side. Mons Graupius was a historic battle, a shattering blow to Caledonian resistance and morale. It also marks a turning point in Roman warfare as the first known encounter where fighting was entrusted to auxiliaries alone: the legions were kept in reserve in case of emergency. So successfully were they integrated into the Roman army, so imbued with Roman military skill, training and discipline, that auxiliary soldiers, of provincial not Roman origin, now played a key role in the defensive strategy of the Roman Empire, and the legions henceforth shouldered less and less of the burden of front-line warfare.

Agricola and fort-building

The careful network of regularly-spaced forts that followed in the wake of Agricola's campaigns is no less impressive an achievement than the campaigns themselves. Tacitus says in the *Agricola* that his father-in-law had a good eye for fort-location,[21] and indeed his network in northern England was retained without substantial alteration until the closing days of Roman rule. There, however, the Agricolan foundations are overlain by successive later rebuildings, and most of the original details (except of the defences) are lost to us. It is therefore to north Scotland that we have to turn for an uncomplicated picture of Agricolan fort-building, an area which never saw again in Roman times the careful strangle-hold devised by Agricola. Aerial photography continues to fill out more details of his planning. He had no intention of entering the Highland mass, but instead blocked the entrances to it with auxiliary forts at Drumquhassle (discovered in 1977), Lake Mentcith, Bochastle, Dalginross and Fendoch, controlled from a legionary base at Inchtuthil on the Tay. Behind this forward line was another row of forts (Ardoch, Strageath, Bertha, Cardean and Stracathro), linked by a road between them and no doubt by further roads to supply-installations on the coast. Strageath stood at the pivot of a remarkable signalling system, with eleven towers known in an eight mile stretch to the east, and a more widely spaced set southwards to the fort at Ardoch. It is a system which bears the hallmark of a general who had thought out in detail the logistics of policing this difficult terrain, and who had every intention of making it work. That it was never fully put to the test was not due to faulty planning: disaster on the Danube later in the 80s caused massive troop withdrawals, and Agricola's grand plan was never brought to fruition.

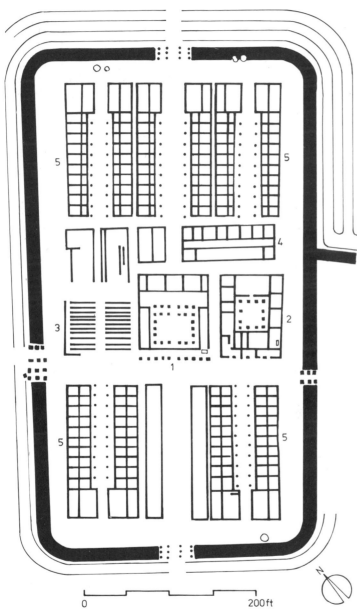

39. Plan of the fort at Fendoch, with
principia (1), commandant's house (2),
granaries (3), hospital (4), and barracks (5).
Three of the gates which were of timber,
have a single passage flanked by guardrooms
and towers above, the other lacks guardrooms.
The circles shown in or near the rampart-
mound represent ovens.

The classic example of an Agricolan fort in Scotland is still that at Fendoch, excavated over forty years ago by Sir Ian Richmond. Some details of the plan, which was reconstructed by selective trenching as at Hod Hill, are missing, but overall it cannot be far wide of the mark. Built in 82 or 83 and occupied for less than five years, Fendoch is one of the earliest examples we have in Britain of what was to become the standard layout of an auxiliary fort: granaries, commandant's house and head-quarters' building in the central range, barracks, stables and stores in front (*praetentura*) and behind (*retentura*). At Fendoch there are two pairs of barracks and a couple of long sheds (kit-stores or stables?) in the *praetentura*, and three pairs of barracks in the *retentura*: 10 barracks in all, which means the garrison was an infantry cohort 1,000-strong.

The 'standard' elements outlined in the first chapter now appear: the L-shaped barracks with 10 pairs of rooms (8 men sharing each pair), verandah and officers' quarters; the headquarters building with its courtyard flanked by long rooms,[22] cross-hall and five rear rooms; the commandant's house with four wings arranged around a central court and a spacious reception-cum-dining room at one end; the pair of granaries beside the headquarters. There is also a hospital here, with ten wards (one for each century) and a long room, perhaps the operating theatre, opening off a central corridor. With characteristic attention to detail, Richmond observed that there was room for four beds in each ward, which represents a capacity casualty-rate of five per cent of the unit's strength. The turf ramparts, fronted by a single ditch except on the more vulnerable east side, define a neat rectangular playing-card shape with rounded corners.[23] One has only to compare the plan of Fendoch with the slightly earlier Agricolan fort at Pen Llystyn or the later stone forts at Gelligaer or Housesteads (ills 48–9) to appreciate that the same basic elements of planning are common to all. Pen Llystyn in north Wales, for example, was built in late 78 or early 79 and demolished a dozen years or so later. The overall shape is more square than rectangular and the barracks are therefore set parallel to the *via principalis* rather than at right-angles to it, but otherwise the differences between Fendoch and Pen Llystyn are in

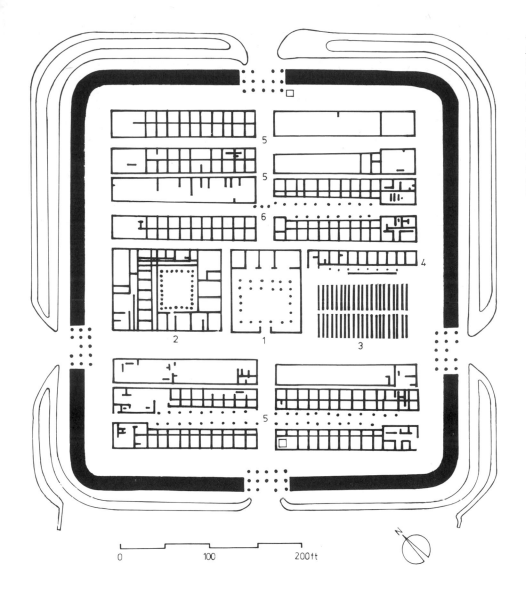

40. Plan of the fort at Pen Llystyn, with *principia* (1), commandant's house (2), granaries (3), hospital (4), barracks (5) and what appears to have been an internal gate defining a separate compound (6). The unnumbered buildings in the *praetentura* were probably stores. The ramparts, of gravel with turf front and back, had timber interval towers and corner towers, not indicated on the plan. All four gates had twin passageways set back between flanking towers. The plan of the fort was recovered by excavation and observation during the destruction of the site by gravel extraction between 1957 and 1963.

0   100   200ft

detail, not in substance.[24] The only major problem is the provision of 12 barracks instead of the usual 10 for an infantry cohort 1,000 strong, but as the rear six appear to have been separated off by a gateway on the *via decumana* it seems that Pen Llystyn was designed for two infantry cohorts 500 strong, a most unusual expedient at this period.

It would appear, then, from Agricola's time onwards that fort-building in Britain settled down to a more or less standardized pattern. But how typical are Fendoch and Pen Llystyn of the forts being built in the 80s and 90s? Until recently we have had too little information about the internal arrangements of other Flavian forts to be able to give a positive answer. But now important work at Strageath, Cardean, Crawford and

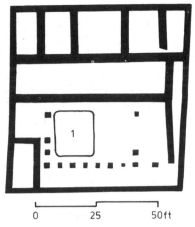

41. Plan of the timber *principia* at Strageath, excavated in 1974–5. The large pit (1) was probably a water tank.

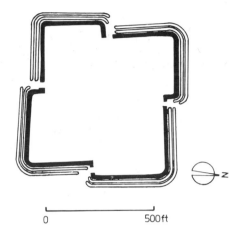

42. Restored outline of Agricola's fort at Newstead (Borders).

0   25   50ft

0   500ft

elsewhere has shown that a standard blueprint was not rigorously imposed everywhere. At Strageath, for example, the headquarters building follows the lines expected from Fendoch and Pen Llystyn, with courtyard (and large water-tank), cross-hall and five rear rooms, but there was apparently a granary in the *praetentura*.[25] One of the barracks had more spacious officers' quarters than two others investigated. The type of regiment at Strageath is not yet certain, but there are only eight *contubernia* in each barrack, which suggests a cavalry *ala* or a part-mounted cohort 500 strong.[26] At Cardean what was interpreted as a barrack also with eight *contubernia* was found in the central range next to a granary, but such a position would be most extraordinary and it may rather be a hospital.[27]   Clearly a great deal of work needs to be done in the recovery of entire fort-plans before a detailed picture emerges of the range of coincidences and divergencies between one fort and another.

43. Another Flavian fort is Crawford, where only very limited sampling was carried out and the restored plan (right) is highly conjectural. The *principia* (1), a mere 30 feet by 32 feet, has room only for a courtyard and a single long room, and the barracks (4) may have had only six *contubernia* if there were officers' quarters. Other buildings include a granary (3) and stables (?) (5), but the positions of the officers' house (2) and the buildings immediately east and south of it are assumed, not proved by excavation. There is no *retentura* or rear gate (a layout more customary in earlier forts such as Hod Hill), but Crawford is an exceptionally tiny fort and may be expected to break the rules.

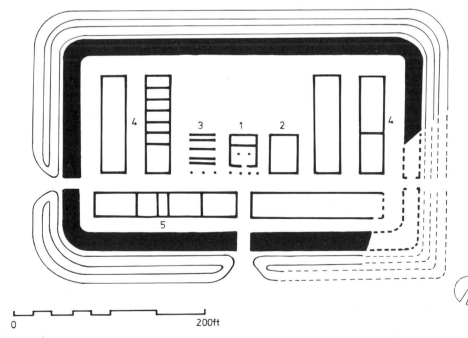

0   200ft

Rather more is known about the defences of Flavian forts, which certainly did not follow a standard pattern: their striking variety suggests a constant process of experimentation, and Agricola himself or one of his more enterprising lieutenants seems to have been an important innovator in this respect. His fort at Newstead shows the most remarkable departure from the standard norm: there the lines of the rampart in each quarter are staggered, forcing an oblique approach to the gates and the possibility of exposing an attacker to sideways fire from the ramparts. Such a strategy becomes central to later Roman defensive thinking, but this is a rare early appearance of it in fort-building.[28] The same principle is reflected in a more common and less radical design, that of setting the gates well back from the line of the rampart and curving the latter inwards to meet them,[29] a device occasionally copied in the second century also. There were also experiments with ditch-systems,[30] and a few changes of fashion in rampart-construction, such as the widespread use of stone bases to provide a stable foundation for the superstructure, or the use of turves throughout the rampart thickness and not just as a facing back and front to an earth core. But on the whole the outward appearance of earth and timber defences in Flavian forts was not noticeably different from those earlier in the first century.

An Agricolan legionary fortress: Inchtuthil

A low plateau above the flood-plain of the Tay was the spot Agricola chose as the hub of his operations to hold Strathmore and contain the Scottish tribes. Today the ditch of the legionary fortress at Inchtuthil survives as a hollow on the east side and the massive rampart is conspicuous on the south: within are 53 acres of pleasant grassland dotted with a few trees. Yet it was here, in fourteen seasons of meticulous work between 1951 and 1965, that excavations by Professors Sir Ian Richmond and Kenneth St Joseph revealed the entire plan of a timber legionary fortress. Almost as full a plan has come,

it is true, from some of the Continental stone-built fortresses, but in those many rebuildings have complicated the original layout and there are now often insuperable problems of chronology. Inchtuthil, therefore, stands supreme, not only in Britain but in the entire Roman Empire, as a superb example of the layout and organization of a Roman legionary fortress at a time when the vigour, morale and self-confidence of the Roman army stood at its zenith.

Construction began about AD 83 and was almost finished when work suddenly stopped four years or so later. The commandant's house had not been built but the site for it had been prepared. The arrangement of the granaries suggests that two more were intended to complete the symmetry, and only four of the spacious courtyard houses for the six tribunes had been built. Otherwise the fortress was complete. The headquarters building is on a surprisingly small scale and oddly set back from the *via principalis*, but is otherwise conventional; there are seven rooms in the rear range instead of five, as befits the increased volume of paperwork required for the larger garrison. The hospital is also a logical extension, round four sides, of the smaller version at Fendoch: pairs of wards open off an arterial corridor through short linking passages, and the larger room in the inner east range may have been the operating theatre. Other major structures include the workshop (*fabrica*) and a building on the *via praetoria* which may have been a club (*schola*) where the privileged soldiers of the First Cohort relaxed when off duty.[31] But the most striking feature of the plan is the serried ranks of barrack blocks, arranged in neat groups of six (one for each cohort) except for the five pairs on the *via principalis* for the double-strength First Cohort.[32] Each barrack has 14 *contubernia* for a century of 80 men, suggesting a more generous ration of space per man than in an auxiliary fort.[33] The centurions' quarters in the First Cohort's barracks are more spacious than elsewhere, as befits their senior rank, and the house of the *primus pilus* nearest the headquarters building, is almost as comfortable as the tribunes' houses across the road. One of its rooms even had a hypocaust heating-system, a great rarity in timber buildings. In the raw cold of a bleak Scottish winter such comfort would no doubt have made him the envy of many a less time-honoured soldier.

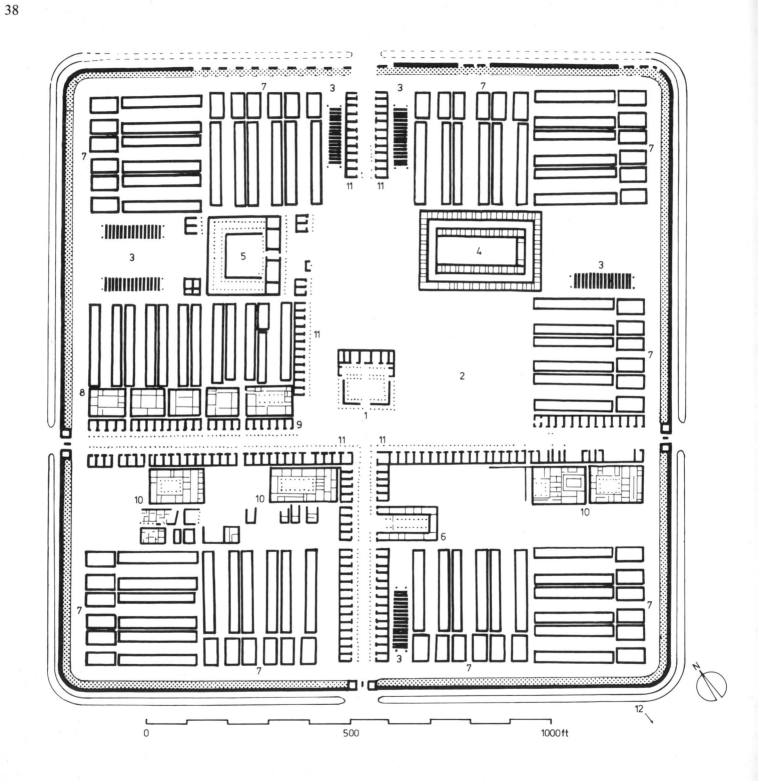

0　　　　　　　　　　　　500　　　　　　　　　1000ft

44. Plan of the unfinished Agricolan legionary fortress of Inchtuthil (Scotland), with *principia* (1) a site reserved probably for commandant's house (2), granaries (3), hospital (4), workshop (5), club-house (?) (6), barracks (7), the four houses of centurions of the First Cohort (8), quarters of the Chief Centurion (9), tribunes houses (10), and storerooms (11). A small stone bath-house lay outside the perimeter (12). Interior divisions in the barrack blocks are not shown except for the centurions' quarters in those of the First Cohort (8–9).

All these buildings were, as usual, timber-framed. The only stonework at Inchtuthil was in the fortress wall and in the baths. The stone wall fronting the defences was an afterthought (the turf rampart was cut back to receive it), and a significant one: it is the earliest example of a stone-walled fort in Britain and heralds a change which was to become common a generation later. The legionary bath-house was built outside the south-east corner of the defences, although fortresses normally have their baths inside.[34] It was about this time that stone bath-houses outside auxiliary forts also first became common.[35]

The hypocausts of the bath-house, however, were never fired, and only some of the ovens behind the rampart were ever used. On the very brink of completion came the order to demolish and withdraw: not a mere abandonment but a systematic stripping, to allow materials to be re-used and deny the enemy anything of value. The timber framing was carefully removed and returned to depot: the vast numbers of extracted nails, bent by the claw hammer, alone testify to that. The hospital drain was jammed with gravel. Unused pottery and glass was systematically ground into tiny fragments and neatly tipped into the gutter of the *via principalis*. Stonework was stripped from the bath-house and the stone defensive wall dismantled. Most astonishing of all was the hoard of one million unused nails left buried in a pit in the workshop. The same careful discipline which went in a fortress' construction was applied to its demolition, a process nowhere documented in such dramatic detail as at Inchtuthil. Freshly minted coins in the destruction layers indicate that this happened in 86/7, after Agricola had left Britain, some four years after construction had started: building a 53-acre fortress is altogether a different proposition to erecting a five or even an eight-acre auxiliary fort. The thoroughness of the demolition at Inchtuthil demonstrates that there was no 'fall-back' position which envisaged renewed occupation: withdrawal was intended to be final.

Even the briefest consideration of the mechanics of building a legionary fortress brings sharply into focus the whole system of organization and supply which fort-building, and especially fort-building on Agricola's massive scale, entailed. No ancient authority ever comments on this, but the testimony of the spade is graphic enough. The defences at Inchtuthil required 82 massive gateway timbers, each at least 30 feet long, and 1¼ miles of rampart-walk timbers and breastwork. For the barracks alone the amount of timber framing required has been calculated as over 13 miles. Add to that the timbers, the wattle interlace and the wooden roof shingles[36] of perhaps some 75 auxiliary forts (about the full total which Agricola must have built or started to build in his six and a half years as governor), and you can get some idea of the massive problems of construction involved. It seems most unlikely that only seasoned wood was used for this operation. Forts in southern England were doubtless dismantled and sound timbers stockpiled for secondary use elsewhere, together with unused, seasoned planking: but most of the material for building an auxiliary fort is likely to have been made on the spot from trees freshly felled in the vicinity.[37] Construction work is only one aspect of the army's needs: other crucial support-services include blacksmithing, for the manufacture of millions of nails, iron tools, and pieces of soldiers' equipment; tanning and leatherworking, to provide tents, wineskins, shoes, jerkins and other items of clothing; contracts with both military and civilian potteries to supply the vessels for an army's everyday needs; and above all the food supply, the barley, the goats' meat, young pig, ham and venison, the salt, spices and fish-sauce, the wine and the beer.[38] Many of these are perennial problems for the army of any age, but it was the Roman army which first displayed administrative genius in organizing equipment and supply on this truly massive scale. Many of the details we can only guess; yet the bare plan alone of Agricola's legionary fortress at Inchtuthil encapsulates the organization and efficiency of the Roman army at its peak.

3

The Second Century

Historical notes

The basic pattern of control for the military occupation of the north had already taken shape, as we saw, by the end of the first century. But the ebb and flow of different political and military situations ensured that many of the forts founded by Frontinus and Agricola had a long and complicated history. A few were abandoned altogether; some were deserted in favour of new, adjacent sites; fresh foundations were made to plug weaknesses, apparent or real, in the original network; and the remaining forts went through a long succession of occupation, periodic abandonment and then rebuilding. We cannot, in this brief sketch, trace the fluctuating fortunes in detail of forts in Britain to the end of the Roman occupation, but an outline of events in the second century will give some idea of the constant change of policy by the central administration. The partial withdrawal from Scotland *c*. AD 87 was followed by a complete abandonment about 105, possibly after a disastrous uprising of the native tribes. The emperor Trajan then set the frontier on the Tyne-Solway line, and his successor Hadrian confirmed this policy in the most staggering way possible, by building his great Wall from sea to sea. The original plan of about 122 was elaborated a couple of years later by adding what eventually became sixteen forts on the line of the Wall itself. Hadrian's successor, Antoninus Pius, however, had other ideas about the British frontier: in 142, incredibly just two decades after Hadrian's Wall was conceived, he ordered a new advance into Scotland, and authorized the building of a new barrier, the Antonine Wall. A serious uprising in the mid 150s in northern Britain caused a temporary abandonment of this Wall, and although there was a renewed advance and a second occupation from about 159 to 163, the more northerly frontier and its forts were actively in commission for less than twenty years. With the final withdrawal to Hadrian's Wall the situation became less fluid, but a constant round of troop movements and fort rebuilding went on throughout the history of Roman Britain.

IMP·CAES·DIVI·NERVAE·F·
NERVAE·TRAIANO·AVG·
GER·PONTIF·MAXIMO·TRIB·
POTEST   ·   P·P·
COS·III
LEG   II   AVG

Rebuilding in stone:
the legionary fortresses

The most fundamental change which occurred in the forts and fortresses in the course of the second century was one of materials: the use of stone. We have already seen that Inchtuthil led the way in having the first known stone defences in Britain in the mid 80s, but it was at about the same time that the other three legionary fortresses, Caerleon, Chester and York, received their first buildings in stone. Not surprisingly the one structure which it was not possible to build in timber, the bath-house, seems to have been the first to have received this treatment,[1] and inscriptions dating to the reign of Trajan (98–117) at all

46. Photograph of Roman legionary barrack at Caerleon, as rebuilt in stone in the second century, with centurion's quarters in the foreground, and men's *contubernia* beyond. The line of the fortress wall is on the right.

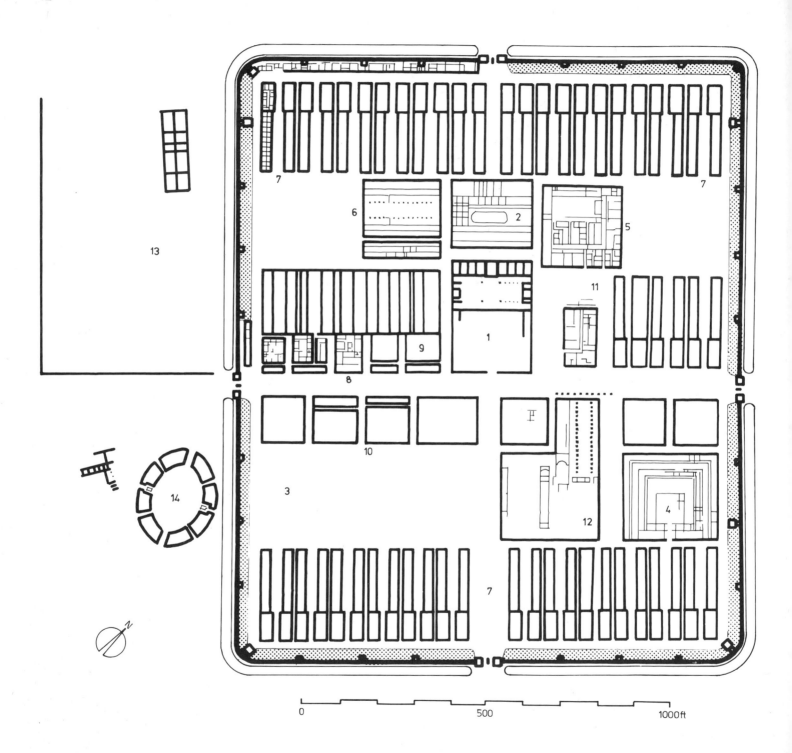

three fortresses,[2] as well as archaeological evidence, show that more rebuilding in stone, probably of the defences, was under way at that time. But the total rebuilding of a 50-acre legionary fortress was a lengthy business, and work was constantly interrupted by the absence of a large part of the garrisons from all three fortresses during the 120s and the 140s when they were engaged on frontier-building in the North. At Caerleon, for example, none of the barrack-foundations in stone seems to be earlier than about 140 and the headquarters building was probably not completed until the 160s or the 170s.[3]

The plans of all three of these legionary fortresses are only partly known, as the Roman buildings lie buried beneath thriving modern settlements. What we do know about them suggests a good deal of flexibility in their internal layouts, which differ from one another and from Inchtuthil in certain details. Perhaps the most significant change in the stone-built fortresses is the position of the commandant's house behind the headquarters, rather than the noisier site on the *via principalis* proposed for it at Inchtuthil. Other differences are either inconsequential,[4] or else follow the dictates of common sense to be expected from the tidy planning of an efficient military machine, such as the location of at least three of Chester's granaries at the river gate (closest to the quays) in contrast to the scattered but symmetrical arrangement at Inchtuthil.

47. Plan of the legionary fortress at Caerleon in South Wales, showing *principia* (1), commandant's house (2), probable position of the granaries (3), hospital (4), workshop (5), drill-hall (6), barracks (7), barracks of the First Cohort (8) and quarters of the Chief Centurion (9), tribunes' houses (10), cavalry quarters (?) (11), bath-house (12), and parade-ground (13). Known internal partitions of Roman buildings are shown except for the barrack blocks: the one indicated in detail (top left) is the only example still visible. The amphitheatre (14), and parts of the adjacent fortress wall and of the baths (12), are also exposed.

Building and rebuilding in stone: the auxiliary forts

By the end of the first century the military situation was sufficiently clear in Britain for Rome to realize that there would always be a permanent military zone with a network of garrison forts, to serve as a buffer between the (potentially) hostile tribes beyond the frontier and the civilian towns and villas further south, and to quell any possible trouble from within the province's boundaries. It was therefore logical to construct any new forts that were required in stone, the more durable material indicating permanence, thus creating fixed garrison posts that could last with minimal repair for a long time. That does not mean that a turf-and-timber fort was ever intended to be in any way temporary (except probably for the campaign forts of the early days), but timber posts rot and need replacing every 25 to 30 years, and it was a more economical long-term solution to build in a more durable material. It was, then, in the reigns of Trajan (98–117) and Hadrian (117–138) that the first stone auxiliary forts appeared in Britain, and it was about the same time that the long process began of refurbishing existing earth-and-timber forts in stone. This last involved cutting back the front of the earth rampart and building a wall of concrete rubble faced with neat rows of small stone blocks, and of reconstructing some or all of the internal buildings in stone. But the change to stone did not happen overnight,[5] and there were plenty of new forts erected in the course of the second century, notably on the western end of Hadrian's Wall and most of those on the Antonine Wall, which preferred defences of turf and timber.[6] Only in the third century did stone become *de rigueur* for fort-building or rebuilding.

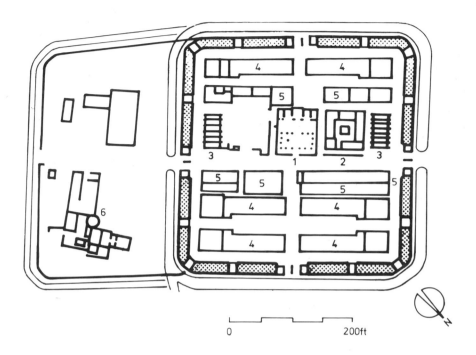

48. Plan of the auxiliary fort at Gelligaer, with *principia* (1) commandant's house (2), granaries (3), barracks (4), miscellaneous buildings of uncertain use (5) and the bath-house within a separately defended annexe (6). Possible functions for the buildings labelled 5 are indicated on ill. 72. Note that the ditch continues in front of two of the gates, where approach roads to the fort would have been carried on timber bridges. The excavations which recovered this plan, conducted mostly in 1899–1901, have been backfilled, but the earth mound indicating the line of the defences can be seen at the site today.

0   200ft

Let us take two early representatives of the new fashion, Gelligaer in south Wales (103–12) and Housesteads on Hadrian's Wall (about 124–6). Both were entirely new foundations, although Gelligaer was built alongside a Flavian predecessor. They differ in size, Gelligaer being 3¾ acres, Housesteads 5 acres, but they were designed for different garrisons, 500 and 1,000 strong respectively. Yet you can see at once that they share certain common features which are 'standard' in stone forts of the second and third centuries. Both have stone defensive walls backed by earth ramparts,[7] with towers at the corners and at intervals along the sides. Both have four gateways, each with two portals and a guardroom on either side. Both have a headquarters building in the centre with a front courtyard, cross-hall and five rear rooms. Both have commandant's house and granaries accompanying the headquarters building in the central range. Both have barracks in the front and back portions of the fort, six at Gelligaer, ten at Housesteads. These and many other examples of forts in the second and third centuries conform to the 'standard' pattern

illustrated by the 'typical' fort of chapter one. The broad lines had already been established in timber forty years before, as a comparison of the layout of stone-built Housesteads and timber Fendoch, both designed for the same type of garrison, clearly shows.

We must, however, be careful about terminology: to talk of a 'stone fort of standardized layout' can be misleading. First of all, the amount of stonework actually employed in what is often loosely referred to as a 'stone fort' varied enormously. At one end of the scale are the legionary fortresses which eventually had all their internal buildings entirely of stone, although even there it is possible that the barrack-blocks had half-timbered super-structures on dwarf stone walls. Other important forts in the second century were also built entirely of stone, such as the base for the British Fleet (*Classis Britannica*) at Dover, where internal stone buildings were still found standing to an astonishing height of nine feet. But in the normal auxiliary fort, even where, as at Gelligaer and Housesteads, excavations have revealed an entire ground-plan in stone, it is unlikely that more than the central

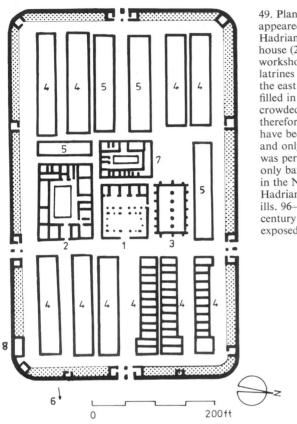

49. Plan of Housesteads fort as it may have appeared when first built during the reign of Hadrian, with *principia* (1), commandant's house (2), granary (3), barracks (4), workshop and stores (?) (5), hospital (7) and latrines (8). The baths lay outside the fort to the east (6). The original ditch-system, later filled in as a civilian settlement (*vicus*) crowded round the walls, is uncertain and therefore omitted. The granary (3) seems to have been a double building at this stage and only later split into two. The whole fort was perfunctorily explored in 1898, but the only barracks known in detail are the three in the NE corner (bottom right). Their Hadrianic layout is indicated here, whereas ills. 96–7 show them in their visible fourth-century state. 1, 2, 3, 7 and 8 are also exposed, as are the walls and all four gates.

0   200 ft

foundations of the central range of buildings: this was particularly common in the forts of the Antonine Wall and some others in Scotland.[9]

We must be careful, too, in our use of the term 'standardization'. It is customary to talk of a 'standard' Roman fort-layout and there are of course many features which recur in all or nearly all the forts of the second and third centuries. Yet the differences are just as striking as the similarities. Some of these differences are due to the different types of garrison for which the fort was designed, but if Roman forts really were 'standardized' by the military High Command we would expect no more than five different fort-types to suit the five different types of regiments available to garrison them. (For the sixth see p 32). Yet the very differences between one fort and another suggest that the engineers responsible for erecting each one[10] are likely to have been given only a general set of guidelines and to have had considerable flexibility of choice as regards both the siting and the details of a fort's internal buildings. There is no evidence, in either timber or stone forts, of a rigid plan or a fixed set of dimensions for any type of building, and it is quite certain that there was no such thing as an unalterable blueprint which every fort-builder had to follow. There is, therefore, strictly speaking, no such thing as a 'standardized' Roman fort, and the rest of this chapter will indicate some of the bewildering number of differences in detail between one fort and another.

range was ever constructed in stone to roof-level, and even there half-timbered construction may have been frequently employed. Barracks, even when stone footings survive, probably always had half-timbered super structures, and there are numerous examples of 'stone' forts which have stone defences and the central range in 'stone' but where the barracks remain of timber throughout the fort's entire life.[8] Finally, at the lower end of the scale, are the forts which have earth and timber defences and barracks of timber, and only use stonework for the

50. Photograph of the east corner of the Roman legionary fortress at York, early third century AD. The curtain wall still stands to a spectacular height of 15 feet, as far as the moulded flat slab on which the parapet rested (foreground). The stone defences of auxiliary forts may have been three feet or so lower, but none survives as high as York's.

Some aspects of auxiliary forts in the second century

In broad terms of overall planning, nearly every fort conforms to a standard square or rectangular outline with rounded corners and is divided internally into three portions with headquarters building, granaries and commandant's house in the central portion. The only significant departure from this pattern in a second-century fort in Britain is the *Classis Britannica* base at Dover, where the buildings are arranged on the long axis of a rectangular fort rather than on the short axis, and there was no *retentura* behind the main administrative buildings.[11] Otherwise the only features of overall planning which call for comment concern granaries and baths. A few forts are known with granaries outside the central range, but many of these were either subsidiary store-buildings in addition to those in the middle of the fort, or else were built in late Roman times when the neat, rational disposition of the second and third centuries began to break down.[12] Bath buildings are always situated outside forts until the late Empire, except for a few examples on the Antonine Wall which are found tucked away inside one corner of the fort defences.[13]

The stone defences of forts in the second century do not vary much from one another,[14] except in gateways. Four is the normal number, except for the forts built astride Hadrian's Wall which were provided with a couple of extra postern gates on the line of the *via quintana*.[15] Double passageways are normal, but sometimes one or more gates have only a single passageway.[16] Flanking guardrooms, on the other hand, are by no means universal. The fort on the Hardknott Pass,* finished in Hadrian's reign, has none, and there are several forts in the middle of the second century which have either no guardchambers or have only a single gate so defended.[17] The arrangement at Caerhun, where two gates had the normal twin guardrooms but the other two single guardrooms only, is particularly odd.[18] The front face of such gateways is normally flush with the fort-wall: projecting towers do not become normal before the late Empire, and only rarely occur in the second century.[19]

Above 52. Photograph of the east gate at Birdoswald on Hadrian's Wall, taken from inside the area of the fort. There are two passageways, flanked by guardrooms, as at Brecon Gaer, but in the fourth century the north (nearer) passageway was blocked up and itself used as a guardroom (note blocked doorway, foreground, and new wall built across the former portal, right of centre). The springer stone for one of the arches is visible at far left.

51, 53. Photographs of (above) the south gate and (right) the west gate of the fort at Brecon Gaer, Wales, as rebuilt in stone during the second century. Both have double passageways flanked by guardrooms, and a drain is visible running below one of the roadways of the south gate. The guardrooms of the west gate project in front of the line of the stone defensive wall, a highly unusual departure from normal practice at this time, one which may imply the presence of legionary builders from Caerleon, where the gateways likewise projected (ill. 47). The gates and some of the internal buildings at Brecon Gaer were excavated by Sir Mortimer Wheeler in 1924–5.

0   100   200ft

54. Plans of headquarters buildings at (a) Brecon Gaer, (b) Chesters*, (c) Gelligaer, (d) Caernarfon*, (e) Ambleside*, (f) Caerhun, (g) Brough-on-Noe, (h) Brough-by-Bainbridge. Second century, except for (d), shown in its third-century state, and (g) which is c. AD 200.

Plans a–f all follow the usual tripartite division of courtyard, cross-hall and rear administrative rooms with a chapel in the centre; a has in addition a fore-hall; g and h are idiosyncratic.

The headquarters building in the centre varies very little from fort to fort. The courtyard is surrounded either by open verandahs, as at Chesters* or Gelligaer, or else by L-shaped rooms which are believed to have been weapon stores.[20] Five is the normal number of rooms at the back of the building, but sometimes there are three. Occasionally the central shrine (*sacellum*) projected slightly beyond the rear wall.[21] The vaulted strong rooms under many *sacella* are usually thought to have been added only in the third century, but some may belong to the second century.[22] When they were lacking, valuables were probably kept in a pit sunk in the floor.[23]

Very few *principia* depart from the standard layout. By far the most extraordinary is the one at Brough-by-Bainbridge built in the 150s (ill. 54h). Here a colonnaded forecourt and timber portico led not to a cross-hall but to a range of four small rooms; and beyond them was one long room and a small office. A few examples are known of cross-halls which were subdivided sometime after the original construction to provide extra office space,[24] but a *principia* built anew without cross-hall is unparalleled. The irregular building (about AD 200) at Brough-on-Noe is also very odd: here five rooms along the front of the building have replaced the conventional courtyard (ill. 54g).

A small group of headquarters buildings, none earlier than the mid second century, is known to have had a spacious forehall attached to the front of the building, straddling the *via principalis*. Only five are known in Britain, and one of these is attested on an inscription alone, referring to a *basilica equestris exercitatoria* or a hall for riding practice.[25] All five of the forts had cavalry garrisons, so this was presumably indeed the purpose of the forehalls, though they seem too small to have allowed complicated manoeuvres. They occur more widely on the German frontier, where they are usually interpreted as drill-halls.

55. The strong-room inserted in the central room of the rear range in the *principia* at Caernarfon in the third century (see ill. 54d) with the steps leading down to it in the background. The room was originally vaulted.

56. The headquarters building at Hardknott in the Lake District, with entrance to the left, courtyard, cross-hall and three rear rooms. The fort wall and part of the unfinished (?) commandant's house can be seen beyond. Hardknott was a Hadrianic foundation not occupied after the end of the second century. See also ill. 76.

57. The rear range in the *principia* at Chesters on Hadrian's Wall, with part of the cross-hall to the left. The building was cleared in the nineteenth century down to its earliest, Hadrianic levels, and later alterations were removed exept for the vaulted strong-room (centre), still intact, inserted in the third century. Its wooden door, strengthened by iron plates rivetted with nails, was discovered in place in the 1830's. The commandant's house is visible in the background.

58. Part of the *principia* at Housesteads, built in the early third century to replace the original Hadrianic building. The photograph shows the cross-hall, entered from the courtyard at left, and part of the rear range of rooms on the right. The masonry platform just visible in the foreground (bottom right) belongs to the *tribunal* from which the commandant could address his troops assembled in the hall.

59. Part of the north wing of the commandant's house at Housesteads, with a hypocaust in the foreground inserted in the fourth century. Some of the floor supports consist of broken columns re-used from demolished verandahs. The paving of the courtyard (centre left) which also belongs to the fourth century, likewise re-used slabs from elsewhere. See also ill. 61.

The commandant's house is invariably situated beside the *principia* and is normally entered from the *via principalis*.[26] The plans that we have suggest that most consisted, even in comparatively small forts, of four wings arranged about a central court: that at Hardknott,* with a single wing and the beginning of a second seems never to have been completed.[27] Only two second or third century examples have been extensively excavated in recent years: a rather cramped three-winged timber building in the small fort at Bearsden on the Antonine Wall, and the spacious, substantial stone house at Housesteads* on Hadrian's Wall (ill. 60d and g). Apparently the original house here comprised only an L-shaped block, the east and south ranges being added later, but from the beginning it was provided with a dining room and kitchen, two heated

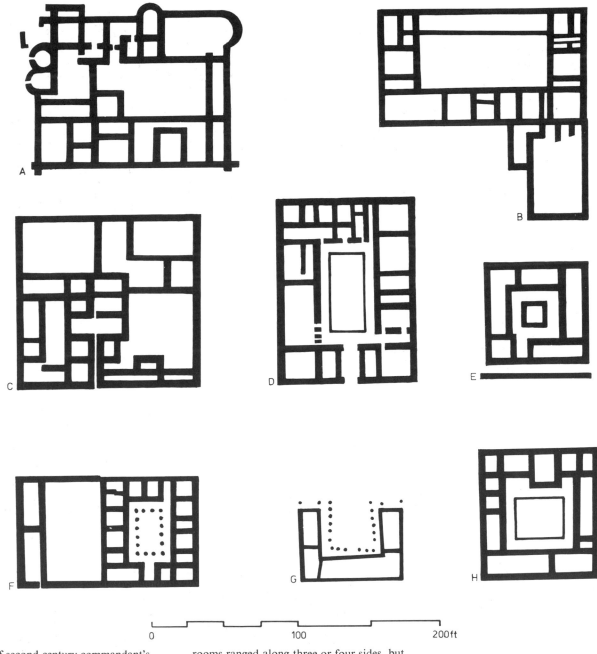

60. Plans of second-century commandant's houses at (a) Mumrills, (b) Brecon Gaer, (c) Caerhun, (d) Housesteads*, (e) Gelligaer, (f) Caernarfon*, (g) Bearsden (timber), (h) Balmuildy. All have a central court and rooms ranged along three or four sides, but the arrangement of c is obscure. The spacious bath-suite in the top-left corner of a is exceptional in the second century. The *via principalis* ran along the bottom side of each.

living rooms, a well-built latrine and a tiny set of baths (later removed and replaced by another heated room). Bath-suites, however, do not appear to have been a regular feature in commandants' houses until the late Empire: that at Mumrills, the largest fort and possibly the command headquarters of the Antonine Wall, is a rare example of a spacious set as early as the second century.[28] Certainly the commandant's house and bath suite at Chesters* is fourth-century in its visible, confused, state, and the fine baths in the *praetorium* of the cavalry fort at Binchester,* approached from a flagged courtyard through a pretentious double-arched entrance, were not erected before about AD 350.

61. Another view of the commandant's house at Housesteads, looking east along the corridor on the north side of the courtyard. The door (left foreground) led to a small toilet, which replaced a more elaborate adajcent latrine (right), blocked up in the third century.

62. The commandant's house at Caernarfon from the north east, with the usual range of rooms and central courtyard (see ill. 60f). The small base on the extreme right may have been part of an altar.

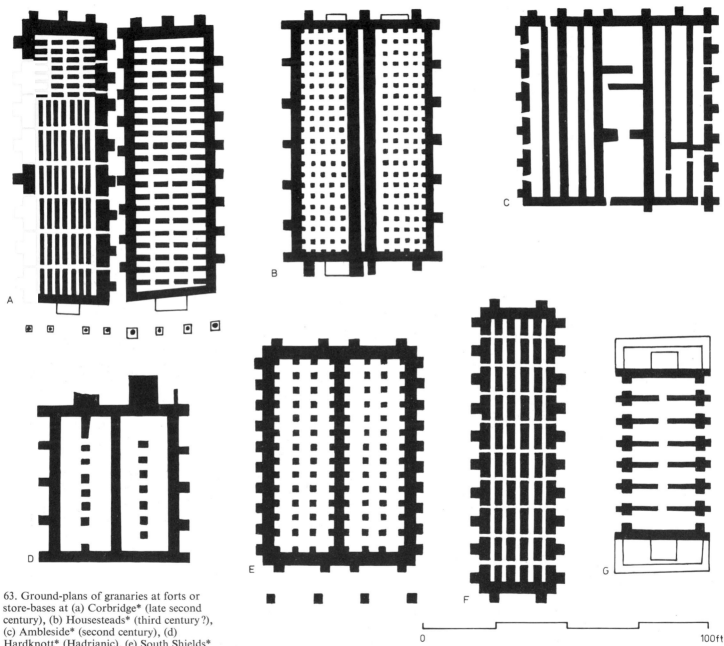

63. Ground-plans of granaries at forts or store-bases at (a) Corbridge* (late second century), (b) Housesteads* (third century?), (c) Ambleside* (second century), (d) Hardknott* (Hadrianic), (e) South Shields* (Hadrianic), (f) South Shields* (Severan), (f) Gelligaer (Trajanic). The raised floors were supported by a variety of methods – pillars, transverse or longitudinal walls. Loading platforms at one or both ends are provided at a, b, d and g, and sheltering porticoes at a, e, and g. The internal arrangement of the left-hand granary of b and the lower end of f are conjectural but probably correct.

0   100ft

Two granaries are also normally found in the central block of buildings (see p 46). Occasionally they are arranged separately, but more usually as a pair, either in one building with a common party wall or else as two separate buildings with a narrow eavesdrip between.[29] Nearly always[30] the floors are suspended from the ground to allow for adequate ventilation. In plan granaries differ from one another because different types of floor supports were used (transverse walls, longitudinal walls, pillars),[31] but these of course would not have been seen and in outward appearance one granary will have looked much the same as any other.

64. Photograph of a granary at Corbridge in its final version in the fourth century, when the arrangement below the flagged floor differed slightly from that of its predecessor (shown in ill. 63a, left).

Below 66. Part of one of the third century granaries at South Shields, with longitudinal walls to support the floor. The fort was remodelled as a supply base about AD 208 for the emperor Severus' campaigns in Scotland, and at least 22 granaries were built at this time within the fort walls, supplanting the normal arrangement. Many were later converted into barrack accommodation.

Below 67. The granary at Hardknott, built in the reign of Hadrian. Originally a single building with a central dividing wall, (see ill. 63d), it was later re-roofed as two when an extra internal dividing wall was built (that on the left); and an eavesdrip left between them.

Above 65. Part of a granary at Housesteads, with pillared floor supports (see ill. 63b). The arrangement probably only dates from the third century when there were two granaries here side by side (compare ill. 49).

We have, then, plenty of information about the principal buildings of the central range, the HQ, the CO's house and the granaries. When we move away from these to consider other buildings in an auxiliary fort, enormous gaps in our knowledge start to appear. Extraordinarily little attention, for example, has been paid to the detailed arrangement of barrack blocks: what we do know, and its bearing on the type of garrison, is discussed below in a separate section. We are not sure if a hospital (*valetudinarium*) was provided for all cavalry regiments and for infantry garrisons 1,000 strong, or for only some of those: apart from the timber examples already mentioned, that at Housesteads* is the only one known in detail.[32] There must have been a workshop (*fabrica*) in every fort, and sometimes it was in the central range,[33] but

very few have been securely identified and some of the miscellaneous 'store-buildings' uncovered by early excavators were presumably so used. We are equally ignorant about stables. Every fort must have had them, for even infantry cohorts need pack-animals and a few horses for despatch-riders and officers. Drains to aid the mucking-out process are likely to have been a regular feature, but only a handful of excavated buildings have been confidently recognized as stables.[34] By contrast another essential building, the fort latrine, is easily identifiable and

68. The hospital at Housesteads, a courtyard building like the commandant's house (ills. 59, 61). A long room at the north end (right, foreground) may have been the operating theatre, but in the long years of peacetime the hospital probably served as a workshop.

69. The latrine at Housesteads, at the south-east corner of the fort (8 on ill. 49).

has been found at several sites: that at Housesteads* is the most instructive.[35] Their sewers needed constant flushing out to avoid disease, and some forts were provided with more or less continuous running water brought by open channels from nearby streams. That serving Greatchesters* on Hadrian's Wall was six miles long, and similar aqueducts have been identified at other forts, or are attested by incriptions.[36] They would, of course, have provided the garrison bath-house (p 62) with water, as well as replenishing drinking supplies and flushing latrines.

Barracks in auxiliary forts: the problem of garrisons

In our 'typical' fort in chapter one, the barrack block of an infantry auxiliary fort was described as L-shaped, with ten pairs of compartments (*contubernia*) for the 80 men in each century, and the broader quarters at one end for the centurion and his *optio*. This was the arrangement found in timber forts such as Fendoch and Pen Llystyn, and it is well documented in second-century forts as well, such as Housesteads (Hadrianic, in stone; ill. 49) or Bar Hill on the Antonine Wall (timber). Housesteads is known to have been garrisoned by a 1,000-strong infantry cohort in the third century, and was almost certainly designed for the same type of unit under Hadrian.[37] Bar Hill in its short life is known to have had two infantry units 500 strong stationed at separate times.[38] So it is reasonable to assume that this style of barrack block is indeed appropriate for an infantry *centuria*, with eight men sharing each pair of rooms.

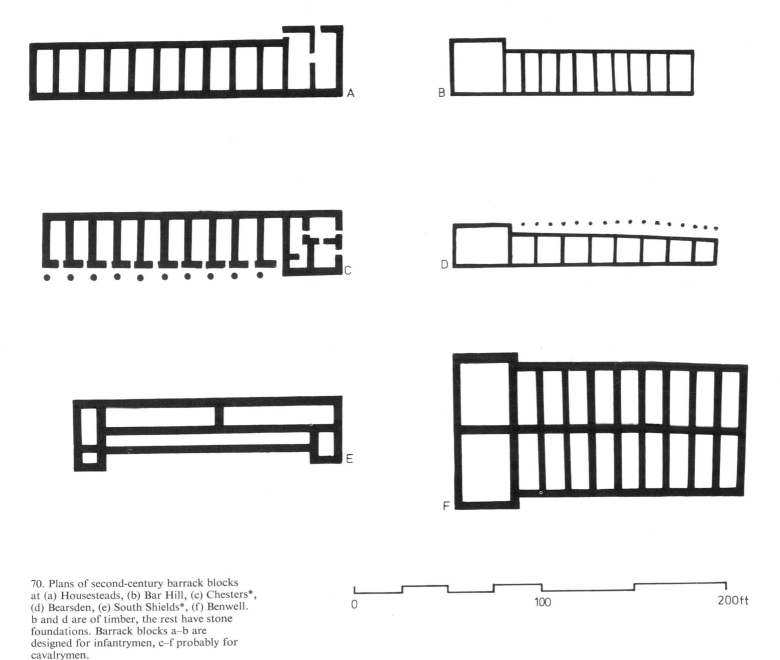

70. Plans of second-century barrack blocks
at (a) Housesteads, (b) Bar Hill, (c) Chesters*,
(d) Bearsden, (e) South Shields*, (f) Benwell.
b and d are of timber, the rest have stone
foundations. Barrack blocks a–b are
designed for infantrymen, c–f probably for
cavalrymen.

0   100   200ft

71. The exposed parts of a pair of barrack blocks at Chesters, with spacious officers' quarters in the foreground, and narrower troopers' accommodation beyond. Only five *contubernia* are now visible – five more were excavated in the nineteenth century (ill. 70c) but now lie below the grass. The drain running down the street separating the two blocks, and scraps of columns from the verandahs lining it, can be made out in the background.

What about a cavalry barrack? Cavalry regiments were divided into 'troops' (*turmae*) of 30 men each plus officers. If two troops shared one barrack, and eight men per pair of rooms was the normal allocation of space, then we would expect a cavalry barrack to have only 7 or 8 *contubernia*. Bearsden on the Antonine Wall is one second-century fort that has produced barracks with this plan, but it was an exceptionally small fort (2¾ acres) and its excavator has suggested that each may have held one *turma* rather than two. We have no inscriptions to indicate its garrison. On the other hand Benwell on Hadrian's Wall is known to have held a cavalry *ala* in the third and fourth centuries,[39] and was probably designed for one in the second century also. The double barrack (two back-to-back) excavated there is presumably therefore for cavalry, yet it has nine *contubernia*. Similarly at Wallsend a Hadrianic barrack with nine *contubernia* (and, incidentally, no projecting officers' block) is also presumed to have accommodated cavalry. Yet at Chesters,* where a cavalry *ala* was certainly stationed later in the second century,[40] the excavated barracks are the normal L-shape with the 10 *contubernia* associated with infantry. The problem is further complicated by buildings of totally different shape

at South Shields* (see ill. 70e) and Caernarfon which are also thought to have been cavalry barracks.

If we *do* assume that infantry barracks had 10 pairs of rooms and cavalry barracks normally 8 or 9, then cavalrymen had a more generous ration of space than infantrymen. What are we to expect, then, of forts with the mixed garrison, the 'part-mounted' cohort? Barracks of different length or different type for the two classes of soldier? An answer to that question is not helped by the fact that we do not even know how many men there were in such regiments: if their infantry centuries had only 60 and not 80 men (p 7), then the barracks in such forts could have all been the same size.[41]

There are no easy solutions to these complex problems: they serve to underline just how little we still know, despite over a century of regular excavations in Roman forts up and down Britain, about many of the crucial details regarding the type of garrison in each and the manner of its accommodation. The answer is clearly to strip an entire fort interior, preferably one without too complex an occupation history, and ideally one where the garrison or garrisons are already known from inscriptions. We do of course already have some more or less complete fort plans in stone for the second century, but unfortunately all were dug at a time when the meticulous observation of today's methods were lacking, and there are many problems about assigning a garrison to them or a function to all their buildings. Let us take Gelligaer. It looks like a clear-cut example of an infantry fort 500 strong, with six L-shaped barracks (the internal divisions, of timber, are unknown) for its six centuries. Are then all the remaining five miscellaneous buildings 'stores' or 'workshops'? The structure marked **5** on the plan looks remarkably similar to what is thought to be a cavalry barrack at South

Shields. Is there room for a part-mounted garrison 500 strong? That would involve housing the four *turmae* comprising 120 cavalrymen in **5** and **6** and fitting 120 horses in the remaining buildings **7** and **8**. If **9** was used as a workshop area and wagons parked in buildings in the annexe, there might just have been enough room.[42] This is a game which can be played with other known fort-plans, with equally unsatisfactory results. Hypotheses abound, but the final proof of the definitive garrison for many Roman forts in Britain is still a long way off.[43]

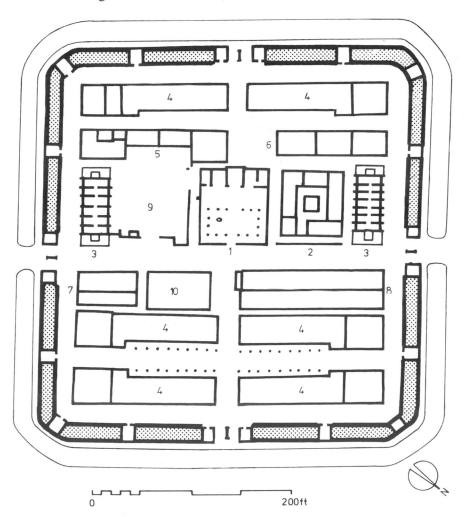

0   200ft

72. Plan of the fort at Gelligaer (compare ill. 48) showing a possible explanation for the function of the internal buildings if the garrison was a part-mounted cohort 500 strong (*cohors quingenaria equitata*): *principia* (1), commandant's hoise (2), granaries (3), infantry barracks (4), cavalry barracks (5–6), stables (7–8), workshop area (9), stores (10). The timber partitions in the infantry barracks were not recognized by the excavators, but their comparatively short length (146 ft. cf. Housesteads infantry barrack, 162 ft.) provides slender evidence that the infantry century in a part-mounted cohort comprised 60 rather than 80 men (see p. 7).

Structures outside the defences

If many questions remain to be answered about the anatomy of a fort's interior buildings, our ignorance is even greater about the nature of the buildings which grew up outside the fort's walls. In many cases the only one known or excavated is the garrison bath-house, probably because in many cases this was the only substantial structure there. First appearing outside auxiliary forts in the Flavian period,[44] they vary enormously in size and the degree of elaboration.

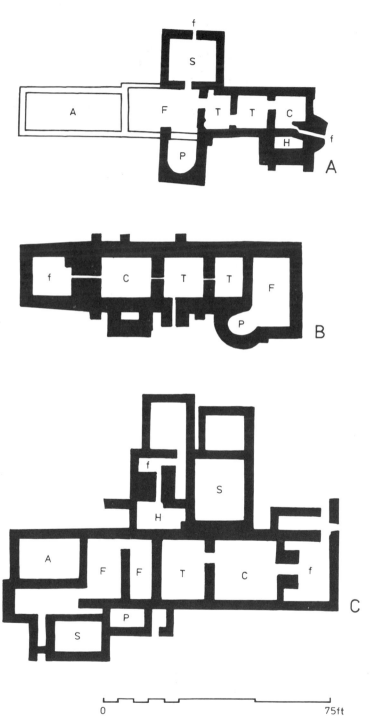

Above 73. The bath-house at Chesters, with the changing-room in the foreground. The niches may have held clothes-lockers. Part of 74a was of timber, not stone (A, F). 75a, which is of late first-century date, served a large fort or stores base (at least 10 acres). The rest are probably second-century buildings, with later additions.

Right 74. Plans of bath-houses at (a) Bearsden,* (b) Bothwellhaugh, (c) Caerhun.
Far right 75. Plans of bath-houses at (a) Red House, (b) Carrawburgh, (c) Vindolanda, (d) Benwell.

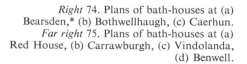

0   75ft

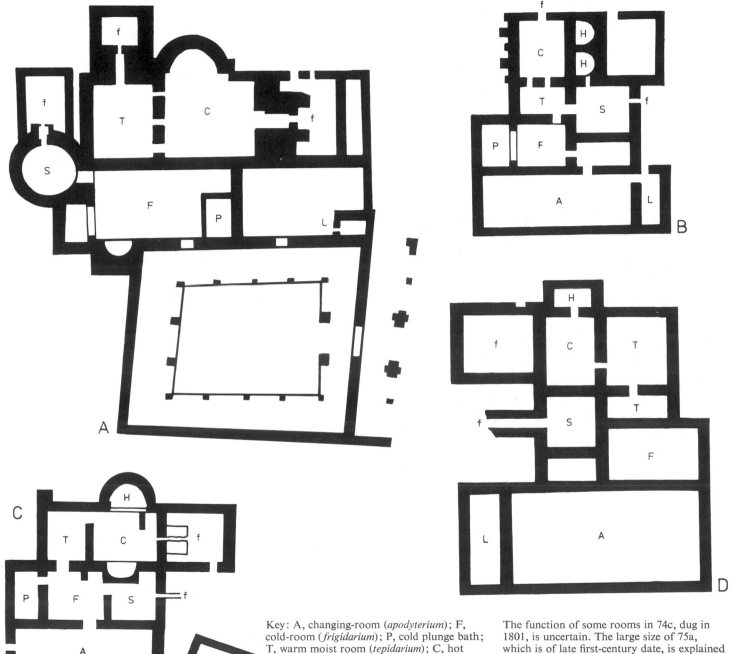

Key: A, changing-room (*apodyterium*); F, cold-room (*frigidarium*); P, cold plunge bath; T, warm moist room (*tepidarium*); C, hot moist room (*caldarium*); S, hot dry room (*sudatorium*); H, hot water bath; L, latrine; f, furnace.
Part of 74a was of timber, not stone (A, F).

The function of some rooms in 74c, dug in 1801, is uncertain. The large size of 75a, which is of late first-century date, is explained by the fact that it served a large fort or stores base (at least 10 acres). The rest are probably second-century buildings, with later additions.

Presumably every fort also had a specially prepared parade-ground to practise drill and other manoeuvres, but very few have been identified.[45] That at Hardknott* is an impressive piece of military engineering, artificially levelled out of a boggy hillside. Another at Maryport produced 17 altars, mostly with vows for the emperor's well-being. All were unweathered, and each had apparently been ceremoniously buried when a new altar was erected, normally an annual event. Presumably weapon-throwing and other skills were also taught on the parade-ground, although outside legionary fortresses amphitheatres were used for this purpose. The size of the arena in these (Caerleon* and Chester* have been excavated) is much larger in relation to seating capacity than in their civilian counterparts, a fact which tends to confirm that they were designed first for military training and parades and only secondly as places of entertainment. Whether this was also true of the only known amphitheatre attached to an auxiliary fort in Britain, Tomen-y-Mur,* is unknown, as it has never been excavated.

76. Aerial photograph of the Roman fort at Hardknott, one of the most dramatically situated of all Roman military sites in Britain. The fort walls enclose (left to right) granaries, *principia* and commandant's house. The parade ground (arrowed) lies 200 yards to the east.

77. Aerial photograph of the Roman amphitheatre outside the legionary fortress at Caerleon (see ill. 47). Constructed about AD 80 and therefore roughly contemporary with the Colosseum in Rome, the amphitheatre consisted of an oval arena surrounded by wooden seats which were erected on earth banks. The banks were encased in masonry retaining walls, and the entrance passages to the arena (the breaks in the bank) were vaulted over and the seating carried above. The amphitheatre, the only completely excavated example in Britain, was dug in 1926–7 by Sir Mortimer Wheeler. Immediately beyond it is the line of the fortress defences. Caerleon church (centre right) stands approximately at the centre of the fortress on the site of the *principia*.

78. East entrance to the amphitheatre outside the legionary fortress at Chester. Note the worn steps on either side which led up to an officers' box suspended over the passage, and the well-preserved door ar the far end leading into the arena. Only half of this amphitheatre has been excavated, during the 1960's. The rest lies buried beyond the modern retaining wall in the background.

Bath-house, parade-ground and amphitheatre where it existed were structures under the direct control of the military authorities. The buildings of the civilian settlement which inevitably grew up round nearly every fort may also have been, even if some control of their own affairs was left to the civilians: we know from inscriptions at some places[46] that the villagers (*vicani*) were organized as a separate unit, electing their own magistrates and enjoying some measure of self-government. Little is known about these civilian settlements in detail. Their heyday seems to have been in the third and early fourth centuries, and some villages were very extensive with building foundations of stone at that period: that at Vindolanda*

near Hadrian's Wall, the only one extensively explored, seems to have been laid out in stone rather earlier than most (*c.* 160–70). Others during the second century seem to have contained modest rectangular houses and shops built of timber; anything more pretentious is usually called an inn (*mansio*), for visitors both civilian and (if the CO's house could not accommodate them) military.[47] Most villagers made their living out of services of one kind or another for soldiers: industrial activity such as metal-working, shoe-making and tanning is frequently found in them.[48] Some of these settlements are known to have had their own earthen banks, perhaps more as boundary markers than as serious lines of defence.[49]

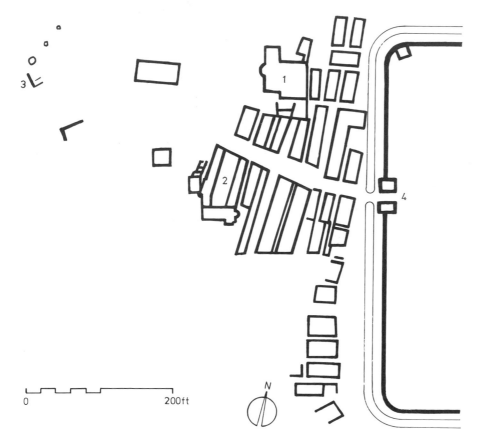

0   200ft

79. Plan of the civilian settlement at Vindolanda, as exposed by excavations since 1968, including the bath-house (see ill. 75c) (1), the inn or *mansio* (2), and various tanks and wells (3). The rest of the buildings were shops, houses, or workshops. Evidence has been discovered here for various industries, including iron and bronze-working, lime-burning, spinning and weaving, and possibly brewing. The west side of the fort is also shown, here in its final phase after rebuilding about AD 300. The west gate, (4), has projecting gate towers (p. 78). The small rectangular buildings nearest the fort ditch also belong to this later period.

80. The *mansio* (inn) at Vindolanda, seen from the south, with the hypocaust of the hot room in the small bath-suite in the foreground. The stone paving-flags of its floor are partly in position, as well as the supports below. The underfloor flues are blackened from use. Beyond is the courtyard around which guest rooms and a toilet are arranged. By the fourth century the inn had fallen into disuse and was covered by other, humbler structures, now removed.

4
The Third and Fourth Centuries

Army changes in the third century

The Roman army was not a static institution. The neat distinction between legionaries and auxiliaries which had been devised in the first century did not last for ever. We have already seen how the auxiliaries had begun to take over, before the end of the first century, as the principal fighting force of the Roman army. The permanent bases of the legions during the second century were a long way from the frontiers; much of a legionary soldier's time was spent away from the fortress, and that in fort-building rather than in fighting.[1] When Roman citizenship was granted to all provincials early in the third century,[2] what had hitherto been a distinction between legionary and auxiliary also disappeared. In the course of the third century the legion became more and more obsolete as an army regiment, and the evidence from Chester and Caerleon shows that the fortresses there were abandoned about the end of that century.[3] The legions were broken up into smaller vexillation units, a size in which they had often operated during the third century, and they were never again to act as a composite force of over 5,000 men.[4]

The declining importance of the legions was matched during the third century by the increasing role played by irregular units of light-armed infantry and cavalry, known respectively as *numeri* and *cunei*. Just as the auxiliary regiments had themselves originally been raised in what were then the fringes of the Roman Empire, so the *numeri* and *cunei* were also conscripted among the peoples of the frontier regions, both inside and outside the actual boundaries. They first make an appearance early in the second century, but our evidence for them in Britain is not until the third century.[5] In contrast to auxiliaries, fresh recruits for these units seem to have been drafted from the original homelands and not from the local population where they were currently stationed. They were commanded by their own tribal leaders and not by career diplomats from the Roman civil service. Some of these units seem to have had specialist skills, such as the *numerus* of Tigris boatmen from Mesopotamia who were stationed at South Shields in the fourth century; they were presumably capable of negotiating the shoals in an undredged river Tyne and ensuring that supply vessels

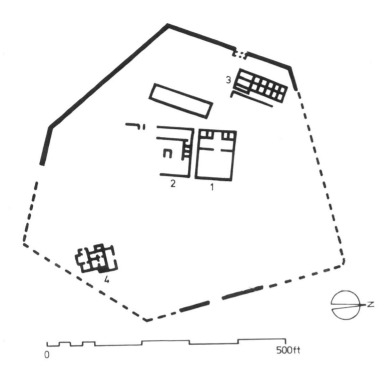

81. Plan of Bewcastle, laid out in the late
second or early third century, with *principia*
(1) and commandant's house (2). The bath-
house (4) belonged to the smaller Hadrianic
fort on the site, and was then incorporated
within the later defences. The barrack (3) was
built in the late third century (its plan is
partly conjectural), when the mound backing
the stone defences was removed.

Forts of the third century (200–275): the use of artillery

By the end of the second century most of the forts
of Roman Britain were already established, and what
occupied much of the third century was the upkeep and
reconstruction of dilapidated buildings. Sometimes a total
rebuilding was necessary, but the new forts normally
followed much the same lines as their predecessors. One
notable exception is the fort at Bewcastle, 6 miles north
of Hadrian's Wall, where the defences enclose an irregular
hexagonal shape to take full advantage of the hillock on
which it sits; but at least one of the underlying forts,
though smaller, also followed an irregular outline.
Obviously this must have entailed adjustments in the
interior layout, but the *principia* in the centre follows the
standard pattern.[9] Another new fort, although a short-
lived one, is Carpow on the Tay in Scotland. This was a
30-acre 'vexillation fortress' built as a base for the Scottish
expeditions of the emperor Severus and his sons from
208 to 212 and held for a year or two afterwards, but
despite the use of stonework here there appears to have
been no intention to regarrison Scotland at this time.[10]
The defences are laid out, rather unusually, to form a
parallelogram about 6° out of true, and the granary in the
central range is similarly built to match it, but the adjacent
headquarters building displays no such eccentricity. The
timber gateways had been rebuilt in stone, but with a
carelessness that a surveyor a century earlier would have
been ashamed of.[11] Guardrooms are out of fashion now:
they are missing here and at Bewcastle.

Carpow stands near the end of a long line of forts
which were created in an age of attacking self-confidence
when the superb efficiency and discipline of the Roman
military machine met no challenge to its supremacy. The
first crushing blow to morale since the loss of three legions

did not come to grief on their journey upstream. In detail,
though, we know very little about these *numeri* and *cunei*.
They are usually described as being less disciplined, more
poorly equipped, and given less taxing police duties than
the normal auxiliary regiment, but such assumptions are
based on little evidence. We do not even know how they
were organized and accommodated in the forts where they
were stationed, or whether a *numerus* barrack looked
different from an auxiliary one.[6] An inscription from High
Rochester north of Hadrian's Wall speaks of a *numerus* of
scouts being brigaded there with a part-mounted cohort
1,000 strong, but the fort is too small (only 4 acres) to have
held the cohort, let alone an extra unit: either the cohort
was well below strength, or a part of it (together with the
numerus) was permanently outposted in fortlets.[7] Housesteads' garrison in the third and fourth centuries was an
infantry cohort 1,000 strong, but a *numerus Hnaudifridi*
and a *cuneus Frisiorum* also turn up on contemporary
inscriptions there: we have no idea how they were accommodated.[8] Again the answers must await the verdict of the
spade.

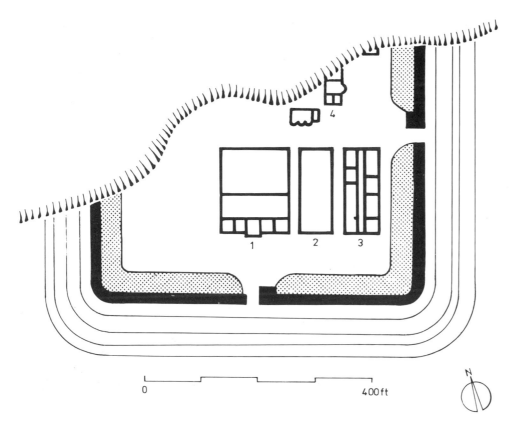

82. Plan of the fort at Reculver, half of which has now been washed away by the sea. The internal buildings, partially uncovered in the 1960's but subsequently backfilled, include the *principia* (1), a building of uncertain purpose (2), a barrack block of unorthodox arrangement (3), and two tiny internal bath-houses (4). The gates appear to have been defended by only a single guardroom and tower. The battered remains of the stone defences still survive.

in Germany under Augustus was a massive barbarian onslaught on the Danube frontier in the 160s but it was only during the third century that a major shift occurred in Rome's basic military strategy. The forts of the first and second century were designed as bases for offensive: their garrisons were trained to fight in the open, and the forts themselves, with their comparatively slight ramparts were intended to be defended only in moments of dire extremity. In the course of the third century, we begin to see a change, and forts were equipped for almost the first time with really substantial defences. We can detect the shift of emphasis first in a pair of forts erected not in the north but on the south-east shores of England. Except for the two rather special bases at Dover and London,[12] this part of the province had not been garrisoned since the early years of

the Roman invasion. To meet the new threat of sea-borne raiders from across the North Sea, a fresh fort was built at Reculver* in *c.* 225–30 to defend the Thames estuary, and another about the same time at Brancaster to protect the Wash. Both are nearly square, with rounded corners, but larger than the normal fort of earlier days (Reculver covers 8 acres, Brancaster 7). Both have headquarters buildings in the centre, but occupying so much space that the *retentura* behind is virtually eliminated.[13] Both, significantly, have massive walls 9 or 10 feet thick (backed by an earth rampart), double the average width of fort-walls in the second century. And the ditches fronting this rampart, at Brancaster a massive 45 feet wide and 8 feet deep, boasted dimensions considerably more formidable than most of their counterparts a century earlier.

The creation of defences on this imposing scale was not in itself entirely new, but it had not been a regular feature in earlier times. The second Flavian fort at Newstead, for example, built about AD 90 to replace Agricola's idiosyncratic layout (p 37), was exceptional for the first century in having a gigantic rampart 45 feet wide, fronted by a ditch 16 feet wide and 7½ feet deep: this was a rare early appearance of castrametation born out of defensive fear.[14] Then, in the middle of the second century, elaborate multiple ditch-systems were introduced for the first time at a handful of forts. One was Whitley Castle* (Northumberland), a rhomboid-shaped fort which takes full advantage of the hillock on which it lies. Its ditches, never less than three, were increased to seven on the weakest flank where an enemy charge could most be expected. Ardoch* in Scotland, an outpost fort of the Antonine Wall, is an even more vivid witness to the steps the Romans occasionally took in the second century to provide a defensible position in an area known to be hostile: on the north and east sides five crisp V-ditches still survive in an astonishing state of preservation.[15]

83. Aerial photograph of the fort at Ardoch, Scotland, from the north east, showing the multiple ditches of the final second century fort (c. 158–163). The village of Braco lies in the background.

The purpose of such ditch systems was of course partly to keep the enemy at bay or at any rate to trap him in the ditches so successfully that he was at the mercy of hand-thrown missiles from the defences. But it is also possible that Ardoch and Whitley Castle were equipped with artillery machines and that the ditches were provided to keep the enemy at a range where such machines were at their most deadly. Certainly it seems that artillery was provided at Birrens,* another mid-second-century fort with multiple ditches since at nearby Burnswark* was a Roman firing range where a deserted native fort was bombarded with lead sling-bullets and sandstone balls, fired from artillery machines in a Roman camp 130 yards away.[16]

It was, however, only during the third century that the use of artillery became a regular feature in Roman fort defence. It was a feature, combined with the more massive stone walls of the new foundations, which demonstrates a shift in thinking: the Roman fort, no longer purely a base for offensive, was being converted into a defensible stronghold as well. At High Rochester,* for example, another fort with traces of a multiple ditch-system, two inscriptions of AD 220 and 222–35 refer to the building of artillery platforms (*ballistaria*), and excavation has shown these to have been rubble bases set in resilient clay to withstand the recoil of the artillery machine (*ballista*) on firing. There seem to have been several different types of *ballistae*, varying in degrees of elaboration; they range from a small field-gun of cross-bow type which fired arrows or bolts, to a large and cumbersome machine, requiring several men to operate, which hurled massive stone balls. In the fourth century this larger version of the *ballista* was known as the *onager* or 'wild ass', because of its vicious kick and the shower of small stones it sprayed up. Two of the stone balls hurled from the *ballistaria* at High Rochester are still visible near the fort.

Other forts in the third and fourth century were equipped with artillery, but the evidence is not as complete as that from High Rochester. Some have yielded stone catapult balls, others were provided in their final phase with new wide ditches which were designed, like the more laborious multiple V-ditches, to keep an attacker at the artillery's most effective range.[17] In the fourth century such a policy was extended to the defences of towns as well.[18]

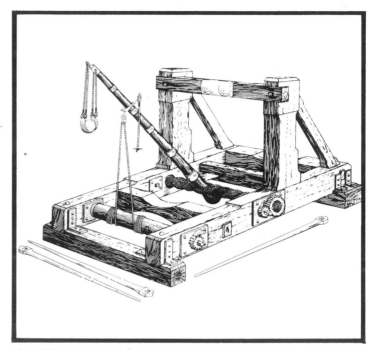

Above 85. A modern simulation (at Vindolanda) of what a small Roman field-gun may have looked like.
Left 84. Aerial photograph of the Roman camp at Burnswark, near Birrens. The three mounds in front of the camp's north gateways are more massive than usual and excavation has shown they were specially strengthened to take artillery for bombarding the hill beyond. Another Roman camp lay on the other side of the hill.

Forts of the late third century: the Saxon Shore

The strong walls at Reculver and Brancaster, and the increasing use of artillery, only foreshadowed the logical culmination of the new defensive strategy which had fully evolved by the last quarter of the third century. The middle years of the century were troubled times for the Roman Empire: political and military anarchy, galloping inflation and repeated barbarian incursions across the frontier rocked the Roman Empire to its very foundations. Britain largely escaped the crisis, except for the economic one, but the pirate raids from across the North Sea, already a nagging sore early in the third century, became an acute problem calling for a special remedy in the third quarter of that century. The insecurity of south-east England is witnessed by the sudden increase in coin hoards *c.* 268–82, and by the drastic measure of stripping a fine victory monument at Richborough* (*c.* 250–60) and making it into a look-out tower, surrounded by earth ramparts and triple ditches. Then came the building of a new series of forts, probably in the decade from about 275 to 285, from East Anglia to Portsmouth Harbour. Even though pottery and coins indicate that all seven of this group (Burgh Castle,*

Walton Castle, Bradwell, Richborough,* Dover,* Lympne* and Portchester*) were built at approximately the same time, the very considerable divergencies between one fort and another demonstrates, once again, that they did not emerge from a single stereotyped blueprint from central authority, even though the idea of their creation obviously did. Gone now are the neat playing-card forts with puny defences 10 to 15 feet high: in their stead arrive forts, sometimes square, sometimes rectangular, sometimes polygonal, with lofty defences up to 30 feet high.[19] The earliest, such as Dover and Burgh Castle, were designed on a rather less imposing scale, and semi-circular projecting bastions were an afterthought to the original

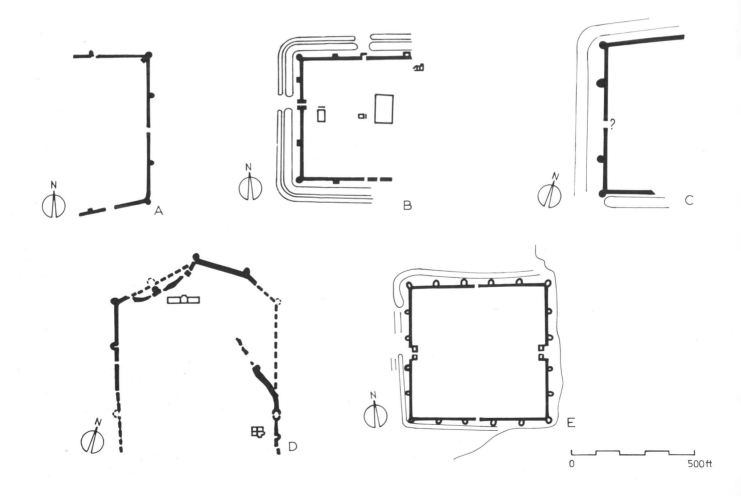

0   500 ft

87. Part of the south wall at Burgh Castle, about 15 feet high, with a corner bastion at the far end.

Left 86. Plans of the late third century forts at (a) Burgh Castle,* (b) Richborough,* (c) Bradwell, (d) Lympne,* (e) Portchester.* The stone buildings in side b and d (top right and bottom left) are bath-houses, but the other structures within the defences here are of uncertain purpose.

Below 88. Aerial view of Richborough from the south-east, showing the first century cruciform foundation, originally part of a monumental four-way arch; the surrounding triple ditches of the mid third century defences, and the late third century stone walls and accompanying ditch system.

plan,[20] but the later ones for the series, such as Portchester (*c*. 285–90), show dramatically how the Roman fort has been turned into an impregnable fortress along the lines of a medieval castle. The rounded corners are replaced by right-angles or sharp switches in direction; the internal turrets have gone, as has the earth bank behind the walls; the twin-portalled gateway has been replaced by narrow entrances, either mere postern-gates, or else protected by imposing towers. No expense was spared on these defences: yet within there was not the neat layout of a 'standardized' fort, but a motley collection of timber barracks and, at most, a bath-building of stone.[21]

Here, then, is a type of fort dictated by a different military strategy. The massive walls were partly intended as a show of force, a deliberate deterrent to the would-be raider: Rome was never blind to the value of psychological warfare. Each served as a base for both naval crews and infantry forces,[22] the one trained to intercept the pirates at sea, the other on land. If both failed in their task and the tables were turned on them, these forts were defensible bases with walls up to 13 feet thick which would not

easily fall to the battering ram or the mine. The projecting bastions, surmounted by artillery, afforded full control over the adjacent stretches of curtain wall. Gateways were deliberately narrow, and occasionally elaborate: at Portchester an attacker who had breached the outer west or east gate found himself in a forecourt in front of an inner gate, with defenders surrounding him on three sides on the battlements above. Whether such theories were ever put to the test, we do not know. The forts were designed, together with others on the French and Belgian coasts, to give maximum cover to the straits of Dover, through which every raider had to slip in order to attack the southern heartlands of Britain and the northern plains of Gaul. This, then, was the frontier of the Saxon Shore (*litus Saxonicum*), the shore most exposed to the menace of the Saxon pirate.

89. The south wall of the Roman coastal fort at Portchester, over twenty feet high. The walls also served as the outer bailey of a Norman castle, and the battlements and many of the facing stones here are the work of Norman and later repair.

The fourth century

It would be wrong, however, to think that every fort from now onwards was built on the same enormous scale as the forts of the Saxon Shore. This was a particular type of fortification designed to intimidate an enemy from across the sea, for the only new foundations of the fourth century which are in the same mould as the forts just described are also on the coast: Pevensey* in Sussex, built *c.* 330 to plug the gap between Lympne and Portchester; Cardiff,* erected perhaps about 300 to protect the approaches to the Severn estuary; and Lancaster* in the north-west, roughly contemporary with Pevensey. All have thick stone walls and projecting bastions; the surviving state of Pevensey, together with the reconstructed walls at Cardiff, give us a striking idea of how formidable

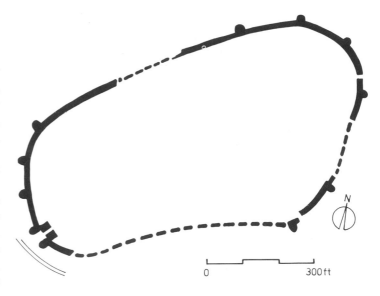

Above 91. Plan of the fort at Pevensey. The main gate at the west end, is set at the back of a court protected by bastions, with rectangular guardrooms flanking the entrance passage itself. There is also a narrow postern entrance at the east end. The walls and bastions still stand to an astonishing height of over 25 feet and owe their fine state of preservation in part to the Normans who built a castle in the SE angle. Unlike Portchester, however, (89, far left), the Roman facing stones are largely intact and required little medieval repair.

Left 90. The north gate and walls at Cardiff, with semi-octagonal bastions, as reconstructed for the third and fourth Marquesses of Bute in the late nineteenth and early twentieth centuries on the basis of excavated remains. The Roman walls were probably rather less high than actually rebuilt here.

these forts must have appeared when intact. The only inland site, on the other hand, to have been provided with massive defences and projecting bastions (about AD 300) was the legionary fortress at York*: but there it was confined only to the river-front,[23] and its purpose was clearly to provide the fortress with an impressive facade, a fitting show-piece for the military capital of the north.

Elsewhere inland fort rebuilding in the early fourth century remained remarkably conservative, and most of the necessary reconstruction did not make radical departures from the third–century layout. Even the entirely new foundations of the late third and early fourth century seem to have been planned according to the 'standard' design of earlier centuries; only their defences bear witness to the new philosophy. The large fort at Piercebridge,* for example, covering 11 acres, has stone walls 10 feet thick backed by an earth rampart, and the rectangular towers flanking the gates may have been designed for artillery. The new fort at Vindolanda* built about the same time as Piercebridge (*c.* 300 or a little before) also has projecting towers at two of its gates (ill. 79) and at least one catapult platform. Even at others where the defences were not substantially rebuilt, the provision of new, wide ditches (p 73), the widening of the earth rampart mound behind the wall, and the filling-up of the hollow guard-chambers to provide solid towers less easily breached by the battering ram, all tell the same story; forts were now defendable strongpoints, not purely bases for the offensive.

The changing role of the Roman fort was accompanied by very fundamental alterations in the structure of the Roman army: the garrison of Britain during the last hundred years of the Roman occupation was unrecognizably different from the army of the early Empire. The new distinction, created first by the reforms of Diocletian (284–305) and then, more radically, by Constantine (306–37) and his successors, was no longer between legions and auxiliaries, but between the 'static' frontier troops who carried out the routine protection of the frontier zone (*limitanei*), and the newly-created, highly mobile field armies (*comitatenses*). It was these field armies who were now the active striking force: they were the crack troops, the heavy armed infantry and cavalry, who were ready to deal directly and swiftly with the trouble-

spots within the province. But—and this was a crucial difference—they were billeted for the most part, it seems, not in the old-fashioned forts but in the towns, themselves safely defended by stout stone walls. The frontier-troops by comparison were reckoned to be of inferior status even though they contained remnants of the old and formerly prestigious legions, such as the Second Augusta now situated at Richborough.[24] These *limitanei* continued to man the frontier forts of Hadrian's Wall and the Pennine hinterland, and indeed the remaining garrison-posts of Wales, but their role was now confined to local police duties and the containment of local trouble. No longer were they expected to launch an offensive and wipe out an invading force of the enemy before it reached the frontier: now it was almost accepted that the barbarian attacker might slip the defences and enter the province, and if the trouble was on a large scale, then the mobile field armies would be summoned to deal with it. The frontier forts were still garrisoned by cavalry *alae* and infantry *cohortes*, just as they had always been,[25] but any newly-drafted units in the fourth century were not classed in these old-fashioned groupings: they were either *numeri* of infantry, or else simply 'cavalry' (*equites*).

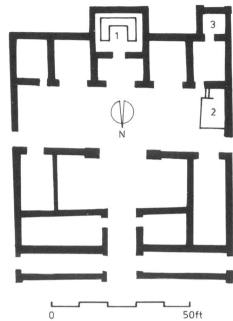

93. Plan of the *principia* in the early fourth century at Vindolanda,* with cellar for valuables (1), rostrum (*tribunal*) (2), and heated room (3).

Left 92. Part of one wing of a substantial courtyard building at Piercebridge, almost certainly the commandant's house. Built like the rest of this fort *c.* 270–300 it had hypocausts, wall-plaster and its own private bath-house. A drain with some of its cover-slabs is visible on the left.

94. Photograph of the central room in the rear range of the Vindolanda *principia* of the early fourth century, with the cellar (1 on ill. 93) in the foreground.

95. Part of the underfloor hypocaust system of the fourth century commandant's house at Binchester, with floor supports (left) and arches to allow hot air to circulate between rooms. The arch on the left was intact when first found in the early nineteenth century but was destroyed by later explorers who, confident of finding buried treasure, ripped down part of the structure in their desire for quicker access.

What these changes entailed for the physical layout of Roman forts in the fourth century we are not yet sure. Certainly the buildings of the central range show no radical transformations. The headquarters building of the new fourth-century fort at Vindolanda,* for example, differs remarkably little from the late first-century prototype we have already described: there is still the courtyard with its well, still the cross-hall with its rostrum, still the rear range of administrative rooms and the chapel of the standards in the centre. There were, however, some extra rooms in the front part of the building, and an extra cubicle at the rear with underfloor central heating: the provision of hypocausts in headquarters buildings seems to have become common at this period.[26] Commandants' houses too show little change. They had originally been designed for middle-class civil-service bureaucrats with little taste for the rigours of military life, but even though such men had largely been replaced in the fourth century by tough, efficient career-soldier commandants, who had won promotion from the ranks or owed their position to patronage, they too obviously cared to enjoy the spacious luxury of their predecessors. The newly-built fourth-century house at Ilkley, for example, showed little change of plan, while at Binchester* a new house with sumptuous bath-suite was provided about AD 350.[27]

Barracks show a more radical change, at least at some forts. At Housesteads* and elsewhere on the northern frontier[28] the neatly planned barracks with their continuous *contubernia* were replaced by rows of independent one or two-roomed units ('chalets'), sometimes partly flagged, and often with stone-built benches and hearths. The officers' quarters are still at one end, rather more spacious than their earlier counterparts. Presumably this new type of barrack-block reflects a change in the composition of the infantry *centuria* or its fourth-century equivalent: the more generous ration of space might suggest a smaller number of men in each, but fourth-century barracks were not universally built along these

0   100ft

N

Above 96. The fourth-century barrack block
in the north-east corner of Housesteads,
excavated in 1974–7; and 97 (below)
plan of the adjacent barrack to the south,
excavated in 1959–60. The stone flagging of
the floors partly survives. The more southerly
barrack (97) has individual 'chalets' with
an officers' quarters at the east end; that in
the photograph is similar, except that the
rooms in the foreground have party walls.
The plans of earlier conventional barracks
have also been recovered (see ill. 49) but are
not now visible.

98. The bath-house built inside the defences of the Roman fort at Caernarfon in the late third or early fourth century and apparently never finished. The furnace lay in the foreground, and then successively the hot, tepid and cold rooms. The structure, summarily explored in the nineteenth century, was re-excavated between 1975 and 1979.

Right 99. The north-west corner of the late Roman fort at Holyhead (Caer Gybi). The walls are nearly six feet thick and up to 15 feet high.

lines.[29] There are other indications that the numerical strength of the late Roman garrisons was considerably below that for which some forts had been designed: areas within the walls were sometimes left empty now, and the presence of small bath-houses inside the defences at several places similarly indicates that no longer were all forts bursting at the seams with a full garrison.[30]

The rebuilding programme undertaken early in the fourth century by Constantius and his successors suggests that there was still a firm grip on military organization and efficiency. Peace, too, reigned for the

best part of half a century, interrupted by sporadic trouble in the 340s and in 360. But in 367 came the crippling onslaught of Picts, Scots and Saxons which overwhelmed the whole of Britain. Count Theodosius came to Britain two years later to overhaul the British defences, and his hand can be detected at several of the northern forts as well as in the towns, many of which were now provided with bastions for the first time. Theodosius worked hard and effected many changes. Some forts were given up. New forts were built now at Bitterne near Southampton, to replace the now-abandoned

Portchester, and at Holyhead,* to protect Anglesey from Irish raiders.[31] A row of signal stations was built along the Yorkshire coast. Some measure of desperation can be gleaned from Hadrian's Wall and its hinterland. At Vindolanda* the rooms in the front part of the head-quarters building were converted into stores and the cross-hall at South Shields suffered the same fate. At Rudchester and Halton, two forts which had lain idle for seventy years or more, new timber-framed buildings were thrown up on irregular alignments. At Housesteads at least one of the rooms in the HQ was used as living quarters, the same may have happened in the granaries, and the commandant's house was split into independent flatlets. Women and children may have moved inside the safety of the fort walls now. At Binchester* part of the commandant's house was turned into self-contained units of two to three rooms, and other rooms were used for iron-working and cattle slaughtering. The comfortable life-style of the commandant was no longer relevant to a changing military situation. At Brough-by-Bainbridge in the Pennines timber shacks for metal and lime production were built on top of the headquarters building which had been burnt down in the great uprising of 367.

Theodosius' hard work had little lasting effect: further rebellions and troop withdrawals in the 380s and early in the fifth century were lethal blows to whatever semblance of a defensive system remained. The final breakdown of military order was nigh. In 410 the emperor Honorius told the British cities to look to their own defence, and the last official garrisons were withdrawn. With them were withdrawn the funds vital for the repair and maintenance of fort buildings, and it was only a matter of time before decay set in. Thenceforth the forts of Roman Britain were at the mercy of those twin agents of destruction, the elements and man.

Notes

References here are almost entirely excluded, except to inscriptions and classical sources. *RIB* refers to R. G. Collingwood and R. P. Wright, *Roman Inscriptions of Britain I*, Oxford 1965; *JRS* to *Journal of Roman Studies*.

Chapter One (pp 5–21)

1. Such as the Numidian cavalry (and elephants) and Cretan archers used in the Macedonian campaign of 171 BC (Livy XLII.35), both of which were employed by Julius Caesar together with slingers from the Balearic islands (*Gallic War* II.7). For the early use of *auxilia*, see Livy XXII.37 (217 BC).

2. It records the strength of a unit which had six centurions and four decurions (and therefore a part-mounted cohort, a *cohors equitata*) as totalling 457, but it is noted that this is 30 men below full strength. Of this 487, there were, before the losses, 111 cavalrymen and 14 camel-riders apart from officers, suggesting that the infantrymen would have totalled about 360. If so, it seems likely that an infantry cohort did indeed number only 60, at least in the third century when the document was compiled (*JRS* lxvii (1977), 50–61).

3. E.g. the *ala* of Thracians (originally from Bulgaria) at Colchester (*RIB* 201) and Cirencester (*RIB* 109); the *ala Indiana*, named after Indus who raised it, also attested at Cirencester (*RIB* 108).

4. Cavalry *alae* of Britons are attested in Germany and Maure-tania (Africa), infantry cohorts mainly on or near the Danube frontier (especially in the provinces of Dacia, Noricum, Lower Moesia and Pan-nonia, corresponding to parts of modern Austria, Hungary, Yugoslavia, Bulgaria and Romania).

5. *RIB* 1778 (AD 136/8), 1792 (AD 163/6) and 1810; briefly also at Bar Hill on the Antonine Wall (*RIB* 2167 and 2172). The reason for recruiting from the homeland, as with other archer regiments elsewhere in the Roman world, was 'probably the purely military one that good archers were born in Syria, and could not be made elsewhere' (G. L. Cheesman, *Auxilia of the Roman Imperial Army*, Oxford 1914, 84).

6. Examples tested by excavation include two of the camps at Cawthorn* and camp IV at Chew Green*; some of those in the region of Hadrian's Wall and the Antonine Wall are also likely to have been labour camps.

7. Most of the identified examples are in Wales, including groups of 18 on Llandrindod Common*, of 5 at Doldinnas* near Tomen-y-Mur and of 4 near Gelligaer*. Camp D at Cawthorn* is much larger and is usually thought of as a 'practice fort'.

Chapter Two (pp 22–39)

1. Punic ditches were almost completely out of fashion by about AD 70 (Beulah and the Flavian fort which succeeded the fortress at Usk are two later exceptions). Other examples of the period *c*. 45–65 include those at Great Casterton, Cirencester and Wall.

2. Unusually there were only two gates (apart from a narrow postern at the north-west leading down to the river): the east has twin passageways and guardrooms, the south a single unflanked passage only. Another unusual feature is the short stretch of mound and ditch (*titulum*) in front of the causeway at each gate. These were an integral part of entrances in temporary marching camps, but they are very rarely found at permanent or semi-permanent forts. Examples are at the vexillation fortress at Rhyn, the Flavian forts at Llwyn-y-brain (Wales), Strageath and Dals-winton (Scotland) and the Antonine fort at Bar Hill* and fortlets at Duris-deer* and Redshaw Burn* (all Scotland).

3. Richmond (*Hod Hill* II, 1968, 79–82) thought that those south of the *principia* belonged to legionary infantry, while the barracks nearer the east gate, which are slightly more spacious and set wider apart, were assigned to auxiliary cavalrymen: but it might equally be argued that the latter should be assigned to the legionaries, who were the more prestigious, more highly-trained and better paid soldiers.

4. Building **3** bears a resemblance to the tribune's houses of legionary fortresses; this therefore may have been the living quarters of the legionary commander, surely one of the tribunes rather than a mere centurion (so Richmond *op. cit.* in n.3, 76). Building **2** is probably the auxiliary commandant's house (Richmond identifies them the other way round). The identification of the hospital with **4** is probably correct, even though its large size (larger than **2**) is surprising; the alternative, that **2** is the hospital (placed as in some later forts, e.g. Housesteads, *behind* the *principia*), and that **4** is the auxiliary commander's house (conveniently situated just across the street from his colleague) seems less likely.

5. Apart from Longthorpe, at Malton, Rossington Bridge, Newton-on-Trent, Kinvaston, Wall, Rhyn, Leighton, Clyro, Lake and Great Chesterford. The large fort or stores-base found at Red House in 1974 may also be of this size. Carpow in Scotland (p 69) is the only known vexillation fortress later than the first century.

6. Three of these, each 120 Roman feet by 40 feet (a Roman foot was 296 mm long or 11.65 inches), were constructed in the normal manner with foundation trenches, but the 420 posts supporting the floors of the other five were erected by the unusual method of pile-driving them directly into the clay, also attested in granaries at the Exeter fortress.

7. Of unknown purpose. Similar features occur in the Welsh stone-built forts in the second century, e.g. Caernarfon* (where it was interpreted as a workshop area).

8. Excavation in 1978/9 has shown that the western defences too take an irregular course, but they are so far unexplained.

9. A normal feature in stone HQs in the third century (some examples, e.g. Carrawburgh, Ambleside* are probably second-century) but this is the earliest and only one in a timber fort in Britain.

10. If so, at least part of building **8** may have been used as an instruction-centre, where small groups were taught the theoretical side of horsemanship before putting it to practice in either the circular stockade or in training-grounds outside the defences. It is possible that **7** was for the officer in charge of the post, rather than an ablution block (both its position and size make the latter interpretation, based mainly on the tanks at the east end of the building, hard to justify).

11. The rebuilding of the *gyrus* was supervised by his successor Mrs M. Rylatt.

12. All are between 11 and 13 feet wide (Clyro, Lincoln and the fort preceding the fortress at Chester). Conventional ramparts of first-century forts are normally between 18 and 25 feet wide (Hod Hill's are exceptionally narrow – 10 feet – but there the packed chalk of the core provided a stability not possible with loose earth or turf).

13. Two were found, near the east and south gates: see plan ill. 33, no. 9.

14. Nanstallon has only a single ditch, and so too all legionary fortresses in first century (except the south side of Usk which has two).

15. Titus Flavius Vespasianus (69–79); his elder son Titus (79–81); and his younger son Domitian (81–96).

16. The alternative is to suppose that the *turma* was larger in a milliary *ala* (say 42 men, making a total of 1008), for which there is not a shred of evidence.

17. But there is no real evidence for this. The alternative is to assume that each century had 80 men as in an infantry century, and 30 in each *turma*, making a total of 1040 men apart from officers. The commander of a *cohors peditata milliaria* was a tribune (*tribunus*), in contrast to the commanders of the other five auxiliary regiments, who were prefects (*praefecti*).

18. In Britain it was the *ala Petriana*, at Corbridge probably in the 90s (*RIB* 1172) and later at Stanwix on Hadrian's Wall (*Notitia Dignitatum, Occ.* XL 45).

19. Caerleon for the Second Augusta, Chester for the Second Adiutrix, then from about 87 for the Twentieth Valeria Victrix.

20. Its discoverer, Professor J. K. St. Joseph, reckons that this camp, at Durno, was where Agricola assembled his army before the battle. The figures in Tacitus (*Agricola* 35.2) give 8,000 infantry *auxilia* and 3,000 cavalry *auxilia* in the Roman forces; in addition the Twentieth Legion was in full strength, but there were probably detachments from the other three British legions as well, perhaps 9,000 legionaries in all. If Durno's 144 acres enclosed the tents of 20,000 men, the long accepted contention that the camp at Rey Cross (Durham), of 18 acres, held a full legion must be abandoned: on that reckoning Durno will have been intended for an army of over 40,000 men.

21. *Agricola* 22.2; in fact most must have been chosen not by Agricola himself but a legionary *praefectus castrorum*.

22. Usually interpreted as weapon-stores (*armamentaria*) an interpretation strengthened by the cache of weapons and armour found in similar rooms in the *principia* at Kunzing (Bavaria).

23. The two long sides are not quite parallel, probably because of a surveying error. The defended 'annexe' to the east, probably a parking area for wagons and other cumbersome equipment, is a feature usually found only in forts founded in what are suspected to be hostile areas: the legionary fortress at Colchester (43–9) had one, and so do many first- and second-century forts in Scotland.

24. e.g. the *principia* lacks the 'weapon-stores' and the hospital has a verandah along one side rather than a central corridor.

25. The rest of the central range is so far unexplored. The *principia* also has rather rudimentary rooms flanking the courtyard.

26. Allowing the normal seven or eight men per pair of rooms this gives room for about 60 or so men, that is two troops (*turmae*) of cavalry or else an infantry century of a part-mounted regiment *if* its strength was indeed only 60 (see p 7).

27. The *contubernia* were undivided and there was a verandah along one side, a plan not unlike the hospital at Pen Llystyn. The other barracks at Cardean have ten *contubernia*, divided by partitions into the usual pair of rooms, but with an extra partition too, interpreted as an eavesdrip, an unusual feature which recurs in second-century stone

barracks at Birrens.

28. A similar layout is suspected at Castledykes and at Tassiesholm.

29. Examples at Elslack, Oakwood, Caermote, Bochastle, Milton.

30. The outer ditch sometimes curves in to join the inner at gateways (e.g. Pen Llystyn, Crawford, Cardean, Hayton and elsewhere), but there were normally only at most two ditches: the four ditches on the east side at Strageath, and the three widely spaced ditches of the east defences at Cardean (overall span 150 feet), are exceptional.

31. Richmond identified it as a drill-hall and weapon-training area (*basilica exercitatoria*) but its dimensions are rather small for such a purpose.

32. The extra pair with different arrangement next to the *principia* are thought to have been for the veterans (retired soldiers) who still opted for active service.

33. But the *optio* (second-in-command), thought to have shared the centurion's quarters in auxiliary forts, may have been quartered here, and so too the cavalry contingent, whose members were for book-keeping purposes allotted to centuries: they, however, numbered only 120 in all. Stables at Inchtuthil were not positively identified.

34. Now located at all three of the permanent stone legionary fortresses, York, Chester and Caerleon*, and widely known from the Continental fortresses. See also chapter 3, note 1. The baths at Inchtuthil are, however, very small, and a larger internal one may have been planned for one of the vacant spaces.

35. Securely dated Flavian examples include those at Castell Collen, Ribchester, Melandra Castle, Slack, Red House and Newstead.

36. Thatch is unlikely to have been used, because of its obvious vulnerability to fire missiles lobbed into a fort by an enemy.

37. 'Green' unseasoned timber has been detected archaeologically in one of the forts built in the 90s at Vindolanda, just south of Hadrian's Wall.

38. All these are listed in the food-order on wooden writing tablets from Vindolanda found in 1973: a unique discovery from Britain and one which gives us a rare glimpse at the paperwork of Roman army organization.

Chapter Three (pp 40–67)

1. At Caerleon* c. 85–90, at Chester possibly as early as the foundation (c. 76–8). Stone bath-buildings within the defences of otherwise timber fortresses seem to have been the norm even earlier, e.g. Exeter and probably Usk.

2. *RIB* 330 (Caerleon, AD 100, ill. 45), 464 (Chester, 102/17), 665 (York, 107/8).

3. But Caerleon may have lagged behind the other two: the *praetorium* at Chester was laid out in stone in the 80s and finished early in the second century, and barracks in several different parts of the fortress were rebuilt in stone c. 100–120. At York stone barracks may have been even earlier: a coin-hoard under a barrack partition wall in Blake Street was of Vespasianic and other late first-century issues.

4. The arrangement of barracks at Inchtuthil in groups of six is replaced by a continuous arrangement of 24 barracks parallel to one another at each end of the Caerleon* fortress, and by a similar disposition at Chester, except that the bath-house interrupts the line at the south end. Another minor divergence of detail is that the Caerleon barracks* are known to have had twelve *contubernia*, Chester's eleven, both less than at Inchtuthil, but all providing more spacious conditions than their auxiliary equivalents.

5. Very few turf-and-timber auxiliary forts are known for certain to have received stone walls as early as the Trajanic period: Lancaster (*RIB* 604), Melandra Castle,* Loughor and Pen-y-Gaer are reasonably securely dated. Many of the Welsh forts did not see stone rebuilding, of either defences or internal buildings until the middle of the second century, and at some (e.g. Caernarfon*) the stone defensive wall is as late as the fourth century, even though some of the gates and internal buildings were rebuilt in stone *c.* 140. Similarly several of the Pennine forts (such as Ilkley, Brough-by-Bainbridge and possibly Brough-on-Noe) did not receive stone defences at least until the 160s and possibly not until the third century.

6. In fact the Antonine forts in the whole of Scotland are normally of turf and timber, probably due in part to a desire for haste, in part to a lack of confidence that the new advance would last for ever. In Scotland stone defensive walls in Antonine forts (e.g. Balmuildy and Castlecary on the Antonine Wall, and Newstead in Borders) provide the exception to the general rule, even though at most forts at least some and occasionally all (e.g. Birrens) of their internal buildings had footings of stone.

7. In fact Gelligaer is unusual in having a 'box rampart' of stone, i.e. the rear of the earth rampart was encased in stone as well.

8. Examples too numerous to list in full; they include Hardknott*, Ambleside* (both Hadrianic forts), Melandra Castle*, Ribchester* and Brecon Gaer*. The Hadrianic fort at Ravenglass, occupied to *c.* 400, also had timber barracks only, but there the central range has not been investigated.

9. Such as Lyne, Cappuck, Castledykes, Crawford etc.

10. There was no equivalent of the 'Royal Engineers' in the Roman army but each legion carried on its books a number of specialist surveyors (*agrimensores, metatores*) who were immune from fatigues and other chores. Legionaries were expected to do a considerable amount of building work, and a legionary *praefectus castrorum* is likely to have supervised much of the auxiliary fort-building. Plenty of evidence for legionaries building forts on Hadrian's Wall and the Antonine Wall as well as elsewhere comes from inscriptions.

11. This fort (still unpublished) appears to have had a broad *via praetoria* leading from a monumental east gate up to the *principia* at the back of the fort. The *principia* (not yet located) had three granaries and one barrack on one side of it (the north) and presumably the COs house on the other. Lining the *via praetoria* was a row of 5 barracks on either side. This arrangement, and especially the gateways, with imposing towers which project from the line of the wall (at the east (main) gate, semicircular; at the north rectangular), was specially designed as an impressive showpiece of military architecture.

12. E.g. at Caernarfon* (*retentura*), Birrens (Antonine I) and Bearsden (*praetentura*) the granaries are known to be additional to ones in the central range. At Croy Hill on the Antonine Wall there is one in the *praetentura*, across the *via principalis* from the headquarters building, but there may have been another in the central range there too. At Chester-le-Street in Co Durham (a new fort soon after *c.* 140) and Drumburgh on Hadrian's Wall, granaries are also out of position, but the central range at both forts is unknown. The granaries in the *retentura* at Chesters on Hadrian's Wall, removed in nineteenth century excavations, were certainly of late Roman date; the Hadrianic granaries probably await discovery next to the *principia*. Aerial photographs of the fort at Beckfoot (Cumbria) show a buttressed stonebuilding in the *praetentura*, but this too may be a late arrangement.

13. At Balmuildy, Castlecary, Cadder, Mumrills and Bar Hill*. A tiny bath at Caernarfon, in a compound at the SE corner, also appears to be of the second century (ill. 98 is a later structure).

14. Except in width: the stone curtain wall is normally 4 to 5 feet but can be as little as 3 feet or as much as 9 feet. The interval towers of Housesteads and Gelligaer are not universal, but corner towers are.

15. Wallsend, Benwell, Rudchester, Halton, Chesters*, Birdoswald* and Burgh-by-Sands: three of the four major gates opened into territory north of the Wall.

16. E.g. at Hardknott* the least important rear gate (*porta decumana*); at Ambleside* only one of the four gates has two portals.

17. Antonine forts with no guardchambers include Lyne, Birrens and Brough-on-Noe; with one gate flanked by guardchambers: Newstead, and Ambleside* (but the latter is usually reckoned to be Hadrianic rather than Antonine).

18. Such single guardrooms are more usual in the third century (e.g. Reculver*) and at Caerhun may be later modifications of the original stone arrangement.

19. The earliest is Hadrianic South Shields*, possibly because of its importance at the eastern end of Hadrian's Wall. The principal gate at Brecon Gaer* (ill. 53) and three of the gates at Castell Collen (the latter round-fronted) also project: these are usually reckoned to be Antonine. The exceptional fort at Dover (see note 11) has especially imposing gateways, clearly designed to impress.

20. E.g. Hardknott*, Ambleside*, Melandra Castle* and elsewhere: but in some cases the 'L-shaped rooms' probably represent only the foundations of a dwarf-wall supporting the colonnade and are not enclosed rooms at all.

21. E.g. Gelligaer, Balmuildy, Cadder, Brough-on-Noe. A range of three rear rooms only occurs at Hardknott*, Ambleside*, Mumrills, Melandra*, Brecon and elsewhere; some may have had timber partitions (making the number up to 5), the evidence for which was missed by the early excavators (at Mumrills it was admitted that they existed but they were not planned).

22. Carrawburgh may be one of this date. Others were at (for example) South Shields*, Chesters*, Greatchesters, Benwell, Rudchester, High Rochester, Newstead (Antonine II), Ambleside*, and Caernarfon* (ill. 55). Part of the legionary one at Chester* is also known.

23. The early one at the Lunt* has already been mentioned p 28; others include Brecon and a fourth-century ⊓-shaped example at Vindolanda* (ill. 94).

24. As at Bar Hill* in the second century and Caernarfon* in the third (ill. 54d).

25. *RIB* 978, AD 222, from Netherby north of Hadrian's Wall. The other examples are Newstead (Antonine II), Brecon (Antonine, see ill. 54a), Halton (early third century) and Ribchester (date uncertain). Dimensions: Halton's is 160 feet by 30 feet, Ribchester 77 feet by 52 feet, Newstead 160 feet by 50 feet, Brecon 147 feet by 40 feet.

26. That at Brecon Gaer is curiously set well back from the *via principalis*, and what the excavator thought was a kitchen or service block partially fills the gap between the two (see ill. 60b).

27. The Ambleside *praetorium* looks like another half-completed building, but there the fort was occupied right into the fourth century.

28. The apsed hypocaust at Ebchester* may belong to the CO's suite: if so it is not later than the end of the third century, when it fell into disuse.

29. Separately: Gelligaer, Newstead (Antonine II). Party wall: South Shields Hadrianic granary*, Hardknott* (before later modification). Eavesdrip, Corbridge*, Ribchester*, Housesteads* (in Severan form; party-wall originally) etc. See ill. 63.

30. Only a very few examples are known where the flagged or clay floors were laid directly onto the ground.

31. Longitudinal walls are the most common e.g. Corbridge*, Ambleside*, South Shields*, etc. Transverse walls: Gelligaer, Castell Collen, Penydarren. Pillars: Housesteads*, Ribchester*, Hardknott*, South Shields (Hadrianic)*. Transverse and longitudinal together: Halton. For some of these, see ill. 63.

32. One of the buildings in the central range at Birrens may have been a hospital, and a courtyard building at Benwell (Hadrian's Wall) has also been tentatively so identified.

33. For example at Caernarfon*, west of the *praetorium*; but the large courtyard building recently excavated in the *praetentura* may also have been a *fabrica* (it seems too large to have been a hospital).

34. Most notably at Ilkley and Brough-on-Noe.

35. Visible examples also at Piercebridge*, South Shields* and a legionary latrine at Caerleon*.

36. Aqueduct channels have been identified at Lanchester and Bowes*. Inscriptions: *RIB* 430 (Caernarfon), 1463 (Chesters), 1060 (South Shields), 1049 (Chester-le-Street) etc.

37. The First Cohort of Tungrians (*RIB* 1578–1580, 1584–6, 1591, 1598, 1618–9, all undated, but probably third–fourth century; also *Notitia Dignitatum Occ.* XL. 40).

38. The First Cohort of Hamians (*RIB* 2167, 2172) and the First Cohort of Baetasians (*RIB* 2169–70).

39. The First *Ala* of Asturians (*RIB* 1337–AD 205/8; 1334; 1348). Cf. also *RIB* 1329 set up by a 'prefect of cavalry' in AD 180/5; but at some earlier stage a part-mounted cohort (First Cohort of Vangiones) was the regiment at Benwell (*RIB* 1328, from a temple whose latest coins were of 161/80).

40. The Second *Ala* of Asturians (*RIB* 1463–4: AD 180/5; *RIB* 1462: AD 205/8; 1465: AD 221; 1466, 1480).

41. Another major question is raised by the common practice, attested by inscriptions, of changing garrisons: a cavalry *ala* might be replaced by a part-mounted cohort, or a part-mounted cohort might replace an infantry one. How radical was fort rebuilding each time this happened? In the latter case extra stables must have been provided, but otherwise it is hard to believe that barracks, for example, were rebuilt on each occasion to suit the needs of a new type of regiment: flexibility was doubtless everywhere the keynote, and modern, over-rigid classifications of barrack types may be misguided. If the size of the garrison was greatly reduced, the drastic remedy of building new defences on one short side to make the fort smaller (e.g. Tomen-y-Mur*, Beulah, Castell Collen*) was sometimes, although rarely, employed.

42. Another complication concerns outposting. The milecastles on Hadrian's Wall, and the fortlets elsewhere which were an integral part of the fort network, were almost certainly garrisoned by detachments from the auxiliary forts themselves, rather than by separate units. It is not clear whether adjustment was made from the beginning when fort and neighbouring fortlet were planned as part of the same system, or whether a barrack or two was left permanently vacant to allow for the outposted *centuria(e)* to be reunited with the regiment in some future reshuffle.

43. An approach to this has also been made through the relative sizes of forts: Stanwix on Hadrian's Wall, which held the only *ala milliaria* in Britain, is 9¼ acres; Brecon in Wales, garrisoned at or soon after its foundation by a cavalry *ala* 500 strong (*RIB* 403), is 7¾ acres; Fendoch and Housesteads, both for milliary infantry cohorts, are 4½ and 5 acres respectively; Greatchesters and Carvoran, both designed for 500 infantry under Hadrian, are 3 and 3½ acres respectively, and so on. But there are too many variable factors to make overall size always a reliable guide to the type of garrison: the Welsh forts, for example, seem to have allowed a more generous ration of space than those in northern England; and if outposting (see note 42) was common, even the smallest forts (around 3 acres), which seem obvious candidates for garrisons needing the least space (500 infantry), might, for example, have held part-mounted cohorts below full strength (cf. Bearsden, 2¾ acres, which held cavalry, but is not large enough for a full regiment; cf. also High Rochester p. 69). Forts of the middle range in particular (around 5 acres) may have been planned for any one of three types of regiment (1000 infantry; 500 cavalry; 500 part-mounted, e.g. Housesteads designed for the first, South Shields for the second, both 5 acres). Forts other than Stanwix of 9 acres or above must have been intended for composite garrisons. Best known is the first Antonine fort at Newstead (*c.* 142–155), of 14¾ acres, which held detachments of the Twentieth Legion and an *ala* 500-strong, separated by an internal compound wall; Leintwardine on the borders of Wales (11¼ acres), placed half way between the legionary fortresses of Chester and Caerleon, may also have held legionary detachments.

44. See note 35 of chapter 2.

45. Apart from Hardknott* and Maryport, others have been identified at Tomen-y-Mur* (apparently unfinished), Gelligaer, South Shields and Chester-le-Street.

46. Old Carlisle (*RIB* 899), Vindolanda (*RIB* 1700), Housesteads (*RIB* 1616) and Carriden (*JRS* xlvii (1957), 230).

47. E.g. in timber, at Melandra Castle (*c.* AD 80–140,) Greta Bridge (*c.* AD 125); in stone at Vindolanda* (*c.* 160–70), Benwell (date uncertain), Old Carlisle (known only from air photographs) etc. See ill. 80.

48. Metalworking was especially common, especially of iron, and has been well documented from recent excavations at Manchester and Vindolanda; the *vicus* at Malton even boasted a goldsmith's shop (*RIB* 712). Evidence for leather-working and shoemaking has been abundantly forthcoming from Vindolanda as well as at Housesteads and elsewhere.

49. E.g. at Melandra Castle, Vindolanda, Malton* (this fronted by a stone wall).

Chapter Four (pp 68–84)

1. Also, but more rarely, as garrison forces e.g. at Newstead and in Antonine Wall forts during the second century, and at Carpow in the third century.

2. AD 212 or 4. About the same time soldiers were allowed to marry legally for the first time, but their wives and families continued to live in the civilian settlements outside the fort walls and no change need be expected in barrack accommodation ('Married quarters blocks' have been postulated at Vindolanda in the civilian village, but on inadequate evidence).

3. A minor change in the composition of the legion had occurred late in the second century: each cohort was increased to 550 men, consisting of five *centuriae* only. Each century had 100 men, plus 10 *decani* in charge of each group (*contubernium*) of 10 men. What this meant in terms of barrack reorganization has not been detected archaeologically, unless the conversions to barracks at Chester *c.* 200 were connected with it.

4. One vexillation of the Second Augusta, commanded by a prefect (*praefectus*, the title which replaced *legatus* as the legionary commander in the late third century) was stationed at Richborough (p. 74), a fort which is unlikely to have held more than 1,000 men (*Notitia Dignitatum, Occ.* XXVIII.9 and 19). Where the rest went is unknown.

5. Apart from a single literary reference to a conscript of Sarmatians from eastern Europe in 175 (Dio Cassius LXXI.16).

6. The *numerus* fortlet at Hesselbach in Germany in the second century has three L-shaped barracks with officers quarters and 5, 6, 7 and 8 *contubernia*. Most of the excavated fortlets in Britain were not occupied in the third and fourth centuries and so were presumably garrisoned by centuries or troops outposted from the nearest auxiliary fort, unless *numeri* played a greater part in the second-century army of Roman Britain than we at present realize.

7. But Chew Green* is the only fortlet known in the vicinity and the length of occupation there is uncertain. The cohort was the first cohort of Vardulli and the inscription (*RIB* 1262) is dated to AD 238/41. Compare also *RIB* 1235 from the neighbouring fort of Risingham: in AD 213 the First Cohort of Vangiones was brigaded there with Raetian spearmen and scouts.

8. First Cohort of Tungrians: see note 37 of chapter 3; *numerus Hnaudifridi*: *RIB* 1576; *cuneus Frisiorum: RIB* 1594 (AD 222/35).

9. A barrack partly excavated in 1977 near the north-west gate had no more than 7 *contubernia* and possibly only five if there were officers' quarters (see ill. 81 for conjectural plan of this barrack). Below it was part of the defences of an irregular fort of the second century.

10. No other forts in Scotland, apart from Cramond* (near Edinburgh) and possibly Newstead have provided evidence of substantial activity in the third century.

11. The twin portals of the east gate were wider at the front than at the back. The HQ has nine rear rooms, the normal number in stone-built legionary fortresses.

12. The Dover fort for the *Classis Britannica* has already been mentioned (p 46 and note 11 of ch. 3). The 11-acre fort at the north-west corner of the city of London, built early in the second century, had a garrison which included men from all three legions in Britain and fulfilled a variety of functions including supervising the transference of military supplies and acting as the governor's bodyguard.

13. At Reculver the *retentura* has a maximum width of only 35 feet, and recent aerial photographs of Brancaster suggest a very similar arrangement there. Brancaster is not certainly contemporary with Reculver (excavations in the 1930s suggested it belongs later in the third century), but the similarities between the two make it very likely. Reculver is dated by an inscription (*Antiquaries Journal* xli (1961), 224–8).

14. The contemporary fort at Cappuck, the next south of Newstead, had a ditch of the same dimensions and a rampart 28 feet wide, itself above the average for the first century (see note 11 of ch. 2).

15. Not all are contemporary though: the Antonine I fort (142–55) probably had three ditches, and the Antonine II fort (158–163) had two additional ones.

16. Excavation has shown that the hill fort defences had already been demolished before the bombardment took place, so the 'attack' must have been a mock-up.

17. Catapult balls: Risingham, Brough-on-Noe, Ribchester. Wide profile ditches: Ribchester, Castell Collen, Birdoswald, Carrawburgh etc.

18. Best seen at Great Casterton*; also at Ancaster*, Lincoln, Wroxeter, and elsewhere.

19. The forts at Burgh Castle and Bradwell were irregular rectangles (and that at Walton, now lost, probably was too), Richborough and Portchester were square, Dover and Lympne polygonal (see ill. 86).

20. At Dover the bastions are later additions, at Burgh Castle they were added during construction (the upper parts only are bonded with the curtain wall).

21. Bath buildings are known at Dover, Lympne and Richborough, timber barracks at Portchester and the later fort at Pevensey.

There may have been stone headquarters buildings at Lympne and Richborough but the remains are fragmentary (see ill. 86).

22. In fact cavalry regiments are attested at two of the forts (Burgh Castle, Brancaster), but it is surprising there were not more.

23. The north-west side was reconstructed at the same time, but to normal standards.

24. Our knowledge of the garrisons of late Roman Britain is derived largely from the *Notitia Dignitatum*, a military document probably drawn up about 395 and partly revised, but still embodying information of unit postings which was long out of date; it is a document with complex problems which cannot concern us here. The *limitanei* were commanded by a military officer with the title of Duke (*Dux Britanniarum*), the *comitatenses* by a commander of higher rank, a Count (*Comes Britanniarum*); but the special importance of the Saxon Shore frontier to the defence of Britain is indicated by the higher rank of the commander of the *limitanei* there, a Count not a Duke (*Comes litoris Saxonici*). These military posts were now quite distinct from the civilian governors.

25. Their commanders now, however, were all called tribunes (*tribuni*), whatever the size of the regiment (cf. note 17 of ch. 2).

26. E.g at South Shields*, Carrawburgh, Housesteads, High Rochester and Caernarfon* (the last apparently as early as the third century).

27. There is no hint yet of falling living standards at other excavated *praetoria* e.g. Housesteads*, Caernarfon*; and the new commandant's house at Piercebridge*, of which only the east wing is known, had hypocausts and painted wall-plaster (ill. 92).

28. At Greatchesters* and High Rochester (outpost fort) and probably Birdoswald and Risingham (the last on the evidence of aerial photography). The type is also known in the *praetentura* at Caernarfon.

29. E.g. Ravenglass ordinary rectangular timber building; at Wallsend there was a row of irregular separate structures, some of timber, some of stone, but not like the chalets just described.

30. Open spaces: Wallsend (north end of site), Ribchester and elsewhere; some examples of internal bath-houses: Caernarfon* (ill. 98), Brecon, High Rochester, Risingham, Halton.

31. Holyhead is not certainly Theodosian, but its late-fourth-century date is suggested by parallels on the Continent.

Bibliography

AD to the third, Baltimore 1976, paperback 1979.

For the army of the late empire there is A. H. M. Jones, *The Later Roman Empire*, Oxford 1964, ch. XVII and, rather briefer, P. Barker, *Armies and Enemies of Imperial Rome*, Worthing 1975.

On artillery, there is E. W. Marsden, *Greek and Roman Artillery, Historical Development*, Oxford 1969, esp. 174–98.

Two major aspects not even touched on above are (a) the everyday life of the soldier, on which see G. R. Watson, *The Roman Soldier*, London 1969, R. W. Davies, 'Daily life of the Roman soldier under the Principate', *Aufstieg und Niedergang der römischen Welt* II.1, Berlin and New York 1974, 299–338; (b) armour, on which the standard work is H. R. Robinson, *The Armour of Imperial Rome*, London 1975. Also useful is the same author's booklet, *What the Soldiers Wore on Hadrian's Wall*, Newcastle upon Tyne 1976.

A. Roman Forts – General

There is no detailed treatment of the development of Roman fort design in Britain. The best general account, already out of date, is R. G. Collingwood and Ian Richmond, *The Archaeology of Roman Britain*, 2nd edition, London 1969, 15–59.

For the forts of Wales, there is the excellent compendium of V. E. Nash-Williams, *The Roman Frontier in Wales*, 2nd edition revised by M. G. Jarrett, Cardiff 1969, but there is no comparable account for other parts of Britain.

For Hadrian's Wall there is much valuable information in D. J. Breeze and B. Dobson, *Hadrian's Wall*, London, 1976, revised paperback edition 1978, and for summaries, plans and full bibliography consult J. Collingwood Bruce, *Handbook to the Roman Wall*, 13th edition edited and enlarged by C. Daniels, Newcastle upon Tyne 1978.

On the Antonine Wall there is G. Macdonald, *The Roman Wall in Scotland*, 2nd edition, Oxford 1934 and A. Robertson, *The Antonine Wall*, Glasgow 1979.

For the late Roman coastal forts there is S. Johnson, *Roman forts of the Saxon Shore*, London 1976, revised ed. 1979.

General accounts of Roman forts in Britain may be found in G. Webster, *The Roman Imperial Army of the First and Second Centuries AD*, 2nd ed. London 1979, 172–220 and S. Frere, *Britannia, a history of Roman Britain*, 2nd edition, London 1974 (hardback 1978), ch. 11. A classic essay, now considerably out of date, is I. A. Richmond, 'Roman Britain and Roman military antiquaries', *Proc of the British Academy* xli (1955), 297–315 and for a rapid survey from an aerial viewpoint, see D. R. Wilson, 'Air reconnaissance and Roman military antiquities in Britain', *Scottish Arch Forum* vii (1975), 13–30.

For concise notes on the visible forts (sites asterisked in this book), see R. J. A. Wilson, *Roman Remains in Britain*, 2nd edition, London 1980.

B. The Roman Army

Detailed accounts include G. Webster, *The Roman Imperial Army of the First and Second Centuries AD*, 2nd ed. London 1979, H. M. D. Parker, *The Roman Legions*, Oxford 1928, G. L. Cheesman, *The Auxilia of the Roman Imperial Army*, Oxford 1914.

Shorter treatments include G. Webster, *The Roman Army*, revised edition, Grosvenor Museum Chester, 1973, J. J. Wilkes, *The Roman Army*, Cambridge 1972, Breeze and Dobson, *Hadrian's Wall*, ch. 5.

On strategy there is now the stimulating work of E. N. Luttwak, *The Grand Strategy of the Roman Empire From the first century*

C. Some Monographs on Roman Forts or related topics

P. T. Bidwell, *The Legionary Bath-House and Basilica and Forum at Exeter*, Exeter 1979.

R. E. Birley, *Vindolanda*, London 1977.

G. C. Boon, *Isca*, Cardiff 1972.

J. Curle, *A Roman frontier post and its people*, Glasgow 1911 (Newstead).

A. P. Gentry, *Roman military stone-built granaries in Britain*, Oxford, British Archaeological Reports 1976.

M. Jarrett, *Maryport, a Roman fort and its garrison*, Kendal 1976.

M. J. Jones, *Roman fort defences to AD 117*, Oxford, British Archaeological Reports 1975.

I. A. Richmond, *Hod Hill II*, London 1968.

A. S. Robertson, *The Roman Fort at Castledykes*, Edinburgh and London 1974.

A. S. Robertson, *Birrens (Blatobulgium)*, Edinburgh 1975 (cf. review in *Britannia* viii (1977), 455–60).

A. Robertson, M. Scott and L. Keppie, *Bar Hill, A Roman fort and its finds*, Oxford, British Archaeological Reports 1975.

Royal Commission on Historical Monuments, *Roman York: Eburacum*, London 1962.

P. Salway, *The Frontier People of Roman Britain*, Cambridge 1965.

G. Simpson, *Britons and the Roman Army*, London 1964.

T. J. Strickland and P. J. Davey (edd.), *New Evidence for Roman Chester*, Liverpool 1978.

H. von Petrikovits, *Die Innenbauten römischer Legionslager wahrend der Principatszeit*, Opladen 1975.

D. Some Articles

Reference to the enormous body of periodical literature can be found in all the works cited in A–C and should be followed up by any serious student. The majority of the places cited in the text and notes have entries in R. Stilwell, W. L. MacDonald and M. H. McAllister, *Princeton Encyclopaedia of Classical Sites*, Princeton 1976, with full bibliographies up to 1974. The annual summaries of recent discoveries in the periodical *Britannia* are of crucial importance for anyone wishing to keep abreast of the increasingly detailed picture of Roman forts in Britain. Below are cited a handful of references to key sites or major topics touched on in this book.

i) *Sites*
Colchester: *Britannia* viii (1977), 69–74, 82–5.
Longthorpe: *Britannia* v (1974), 1–129.
Usk: *Roman Frontier Studies 1969* (Cardiff 1974), 61–9.

Current Archaeology 62 (June 1978), 71–7.
Nanstallon: Britannia iii (1972), 56–111.
Baginton: Transactions of Birmingham Archaeological Society lxxxiii
(1966–7), 65–129; lxxxv (1973), 7–92; lxxxvii (1975), 1–56.
Current Archaeology 44 (May 1974), 271–80; 63 (Sept. 1978),
123–5.
Fendoch: Proceedings, Society of Antiquities of Scotland lxxiii (1938–9),
110–54.
Crawford: ibid. civ (1971–2), 147–200.
Newstead: ibid. lxxxiv (1949–50), 2–7.
Pen Llystyn: Archaeological Journal cxxv (1969), 101–92.
Inchtuthil: Third Limes Studien (Basel 1959), 152–5.
Summaries in JRS from vol. xliii (1953) to lvi (1966).
Dover: Kent Archaeological Review xxiii (1971), 74–86.
Current Archaeology 38 (May 1973), 81–8.
London: R. Merrifield, The Roman City of London, 96–101.
Brough-by-Bainbridge: Proceedings Leeds Philosophical and Literary
Society lx (1960), 107–31; JRS lix (1969), 207–8.
Brough-on-Noe: Summaries in Derbyshire Archaeological Journal from
1965–9.
Ilkley: Yorkshire Archaeological Journal xxviii (1924–6), 137–321.
Proceedings Leeds Philosophical and Literary Society xii (1966),
23–72.
Melandra: Victoria County History, Derbyshire I, London 1903, 210–5.
Derbyshire Archaeological Journal lxxxiii (1963), 3–9; xci
(1971), 58–118.
Ribchester: B. J. N. Edwards, Ribchester, Lancashire, National Trust 1972.
Binchester: Transactions of Architectural and Archaeological Society of
Durham and Northumberland xi (1958), 115–24; new series ii
(1970), 33–7.
Piercebridge: ibid. vii (1936), 235–77; lx (1939–41), 413–68; new series i
(1968), 27–44.
Chester-le-Street: Archaeologia Aeliana[4] xlvi (1968), 75–96.
Ambleside: Transactions of Cumberland and Westmorland Antiquarian and
Archaeological Society[2] xv (1915), 3–62; xx (1921), 1–24.
Hardknott: ibid. xxviii (1928), 314–52; lxiii (1963), 148–52; lxv (1965),
169–75.
Bewcastle: ibid. xxxviii (1938), 195–237; JRS xlvii (1957), 204.
Carpow: Proceedings, Society of Antiquaries of Scotland xcvi (1962–3),
184–207.
Roman Frontier Studies 1967 (Tel Aviv 1971), 51–4.
Whitley Castle: Proceedings, Society of Antiquaries of Newcastle i (1924),
249–55.
Archaeologia Aeliana[4] xxxvii (1959), 191–202.
Ardoch: Archaeological Journal cxxi (1964), 196.
Burnswark: Historia xxi (1972), 99–113.
High Rochester, Risingham: I. A. Richmond, History of Northumberland
XV (1940), 97–9 (also RIB 1280–1).
Lancaster: Transactions of Historical Society of Lancashire and Cheshire v
(1953), 1–23.

ii) Topics
Recruitment: R. W. Davies, Bonner Jahrbücher clxix (1969), 208–32.
Camps: D. R. Wilson, Ninth Limes Congress (Bucharest-Köln 1974),
341–50.
Timber construction: I. A. Richmond in E. M. Jope (ed.), Studies in
Building History, London 1961, 15–26.
Timber gates: W. H. Manning and I. R. Scott, Britannia x (1979), 19–61.

Timber granaries: W. H. Manning, Saalburg Jahrbuch xxxii (1975), 105–29.
Supplies: W. S. Hanson, Britannia ix (1978), 293–305.
Garrisons: D. Breeze, Britannia v (1974), 144–54 and Vortrage des 10
Internationalen Limeskongresses, Köln-Bonn 1977, 1–6.
Third-century reforms: E. Birley, Epigraphische Studien 8 (1969), 63–82.
R. E. Smith, Historia xxi (1972), 481–500.
Numeri and cunei: J. C. Mann, Hermes lxxxii (1954), 501–6.
H. Callies, Bericht der Römisch-Germanisch Kommission
1964 xlv (1965), 130–227.
Fourth-century rebuilding
on Hadrian's Wall: J. J. Wilkes in M. G. Jarrett and B. Dobson (edd.),
Britain and Rome, Kendal 1966, 114–38.

92

Fortresses
1. Caerleon (Gwent)
2. Chester (Cheshire)
3. Colchester (Essex)
4. Exeter (Devon)
5. Gloucester (Gloucestershire)
6. Inchtuthil (Tayside)
7. Lincoln (Lincolnshire)
8. Usk (Gwent)
9. Wroxeter (Shropshire)
10. York (North Yorkshire)

Vexillation Fortresses
11. Carpow (Tayside)
12. Clyro (Powys)
13. Great Chesterford (Essex)
14. Kinvaston (Staffordshire)
15. Lake (Dorset)
16. Leighton (Shropshire)
17. Longthorpe (Cambridgeshire)
18. Malton (North Yorkshire)
19. Newton-on-Trent (Lincolnshire)
20. Rhyn Park (Shropshire)
21. Rossington Bridge (South Yorkshire)
22. Wall (Staffordshire)

Forts
23. Ambleside (Cumbria)
24. Ardoch (Tayside)
25. Baginton (Warwickshire)
26. Balmuildy (Strathclyde)
27. Bar Hill (Strathclyde)
28. Bearsden (Strathclyde)
29. Beckfoot (Cumbria)
30. Benwell (Tyne and Wear)
31. Bertha (Tayside)
32. Beulah (Powys)
33. Bewcastle (Cumbria)
34. Binchester (Durham)
35. Birdoswald (Cumbria)

36. Birrens (Dumfries & Galloway)
37. Bitterne (Hampshire)
38. Bochastle (Central)
39. Bowes (Durham)
40. Bradwell (Essex)
41. Brancaster (Norfolk)
42. Brecon Gaer (Powys)
43. Brough-by-Bainbridge (North Yorkshire)
44. Brough-on-Noe (Derbyshire)
45. Burgh-by-Sands (Cumbria)
46. Burgh Castle (Norfolk)
47. Cadder (Strathclyde)
48. Caerhun (Gwynedd)
49. Caermote (Cumbria)
50. Caernarfon (Gwynedd)
51. Cappuck (Borders)
52. Cardean (Tayside)
53. Cardiff (South Glamorgan)
54. Carrawburgh (Northumberland)
55. Carriden (Central)
56. Carvoran (Northumberland)
57. Castell Collen (Powys)
58. Castlecary (Strathclyde)
59. Castledykes (Strathclyde)
60. Chester-le-Street (Durham)
61. Chesters (Northumberland)
62. Cirencester (Gloucestershire)
63. Corbridge (Northumberland)
64. Cramond (Lothian)
65. Crawford (Strathclyde)
66. Croy Hill (Strathclyde)
67. Dalginross (Tayside)
68. Dalswinton (Dumfries & Galloway)
69. Dover (Kent)
70. Drumburgh (Cumbria)

71. Drumquhassle (Central)
72. Ebchester (Durham)
73. Elslack (North Yorkshire)
74. Fendoch (Tayside)
75. Gelligaer (Mid Glamorgan)
76. Great Casterton (Leicestershire)
77. Greatchesters (Northumberland)
78. Greta Bridge (North Yorkshire)
79. Halton (Northumberland)
80. Hardknott (Cumbria)
81. Hayton (Humberside)
82. High Rochester (Northumberland)
83. Hod Hill (Dorset)
84. Holyhead (Gwynedd)
85. Housesteads (Northumberland)
86. Ilkley (West Yorkshire)
87. Lake Menteith (Central)
88. Lancaster (Lancashire)
89. Lanchester (Durham)
90. Leintwardine (Hereford & Worcester)
91. Llyn-y-brain (Powys)
92. London
93. Loughor (West Glamorgan)
94. Lympne (Kent)
95. Lyne (Borders)
96. Manchester
97. Maryport (Cumbria)
98. Melandra Castle (Derbyshire)
99. Mumrills (Central)
100. Nanstallon (Cornwall)
101. Netherby (Cumbria)
102. Newstead (Borders)
103. Oakwood (Borders)
104. Old Carlisle (Cumbria)
105. Pen Llystyn (Gwynedd)
106. Penydarren (Mid Glamorgan)
107. Pen-y-Gaer (Powys)
108. Pevensey (East Sussex)
109. Piercebridge (Durham)
110. Portchester (Hampshire)
111. Ravenglass (Cumbria)
112. Reculver (Kent)
113. Red House (Northumberland)
114. Ribchester (Lancashire)
115. Richborough (Kent)
116. Risingham (Northumberland)
117. Rudchester (Northumberland)
118. Slack (West Yorkshire)
119. South Shields (Tyne & Wear)
120. Stanwix (Cumbria)
121. Stracathro (Tayside)
122. Strageath (Tayside)
123. Tassiesholm (Dumfries & Galloway)
124. Tomen-y-Mur (Gwynedd)
125. Vindolanda (Northumberland)
126. Waddon Hill (Dorset)
127. Wallsend (Tyne & Wear)
128. Walton Castle (Suffolk)
129. Whitley Castle (Northumberland)

Fortlets
130. Chew Green (Northumberland)

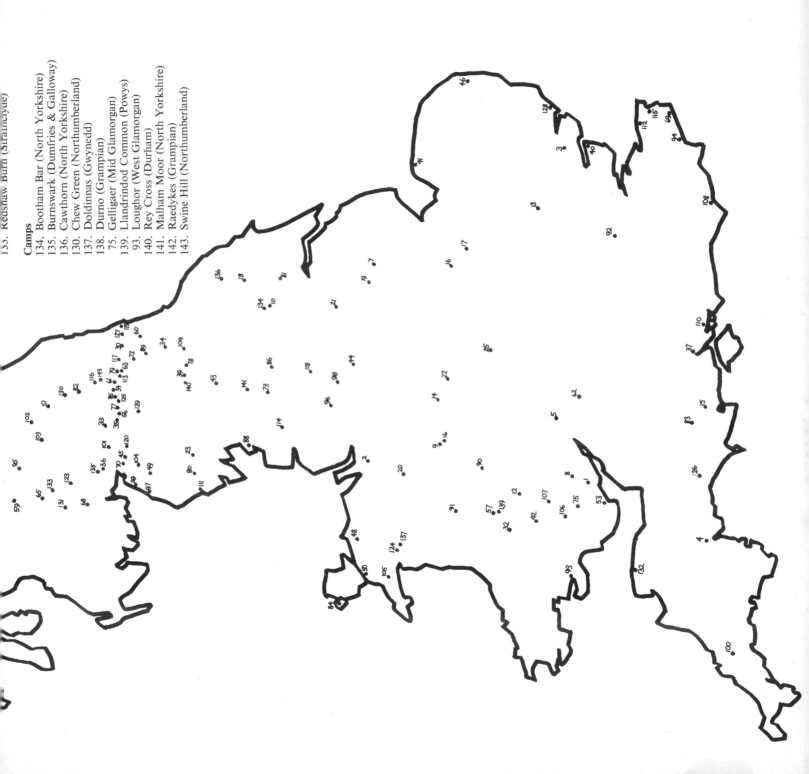

Glossary

ala: regiment of cavalry in the Roman auxiliary army

ballista: artillery machine discharging arrows and/or stone balls

ballistarium: (plural *ballistaria*): emplacement for a *ballista*

bastion: semicircular or polygonal tower projecting from a fort wall

breastwork: the vertical timber-work built on top of the earth rampart of a fort to provide screening for the sentry

castrametation: the science of fortification

centuria: unit of infantry soldiers, normally 80 in number, in both a legion and an auxiliary regiment

centurion: professional soldier in command of a *centuria*

century: English translation of *centuria*

comitatenses: mobile field-units in the late Roman army

contubernium (plural *contubernia*): a room or pair of rooms in a barrack-block shared by a mess-unit of Roman soldiers

crenellations: indented parapet along the top of a fortification, consisting alternately of raised sections (merlons) for protection, and openings for visibility and firing

cross-hall: covered assembly area in the headquarters building of a fort or fortress

cuneus (plural *cunei*): unit of irregular cavalry

daub: see wattle-and-daub

hill fort: prehistoric earthwork fortification, usually defending a hill-top

hypocaust: Roman method of central heating by circulating hot air under the floor and up flues in the walls

limitanei: frontier-troops in the late Roman army

louvers: overlapping boards arranged obliquely so as to admit air and some light but to exclude rain

mine: subterranean passage dug by an enemy below fortifications to 'undermine' them and cause their collapse

numerus: unit of irregular, light-armed infantry

onager: name given to a particularly large version of the *ballista* (q.v.)

optio: second-in-command of a *centuria* (q.v.), below the centurion (q.v.)

patrol-walk: flat area on top of a Roman rampart controlled by the sentry and protected by breastworks (q.v.) or crenellations (q.v.)

postern: minor, narrow gate in a Roman fort, especially of late Roman date

praetentura: the front area of a Roman fort, towards which the *principia* (q.v.) faces

principia: headquarters building in the centre of a Roman fort or fortress

retentura: the rear area of a Roman fort, behind the *principia* (q.v.)

revetment: facing of one material given to a structure of a different material (e.g. a stone or turf facing to the earth core of fort defences)

sacellum: shrine in a fort's headquarters building

turma: troop of cavalry in an *ala* (q.v.), usually 32 men including officers

vexillation: detachment of a legion, normally 1,000 men

via decumana: the road in a Roman fort leading from the rear of the headquarters building to the back gate

via praetoria: the road in a Roman fort leading from the front of the headquarters building to the front gate

via principalis: road joining two main gates and passing along the front of the headquarters building

via quintana: road running parallel to the *via principalis* (q.v.) behind the headquarters building

vicus: settlement of civilians living outside a fort

wall-walk: level platform for sentry on top of a fortification

wattle-and-daub: wall-construction consisting of wickerwork plastered with mud

Some Roman Emperors
The dates of Roman Emperors mentioned in this book
are:

Augustus	27 BC–AD 14	Nerva	96–98
Claudius	41–54	Trajan	98–117
Nero	54–68	Hadrian	117–138
Vespasian	69–79	Antoninus Pius	138–161
Titus	79–81	Severus	193–211
Domitian	81–96	Constantius	293–306
		Honorius	395–423

The adjective *Flavian* refers in general to the period 69–96, *Agricolan* more specifically to the period when Agricola was governor of Britain, i.e. 78–84/5. *Antonine* refers technically to the period 138–192, but is divided into two principal phases of occupation in British forts, *Antonine I* from *c.* 140–*c.* 155 and *Antonine II* from *c.* 156 onwards (in most of Scotland the Antonine II period is only from *c.* 158 to *c.* 163). *Theodosian* refers to the period *c.* 369–70.

Index

Material in the notes and captions is not indexed, but illustrations are referred to by the number in italics.